PRAISE FOR DR. MCREYNOLDS AND
SOLVING THE ADHD RIDDLE

"*Solving the ADHD Riddle* brings hope to families with children who are struggling with visual and auditory processing. It reaches the core of the problem with viable resources, simple strategies, and solutions for parents and teachers that can make a world of difference in the child's learning experiences. With her assessment results and interventions, a process of retraining the brain gives the first steps to opening up a new journey of success. Dr. McReynolds, thank you for opening the doors to many students to rewire their brains and build success with neurofeedback and your many strategies."

—Dr. Jean Maddox,
elementary school principal (ret.)

"Dr. McReynolds has cut the Gordian knot of auditory and visual processing problems! This seminal work of applied technologies, tenacity, triumph, and hope is as audacious as it is remarkable. Dr. McReynolds shines a beacon into the complex world of ADHD with real world examples and applications."

—Jim Swanson,
M.A., rehabilitation counselor, LPPC-S

"The effect of a learning disability is global for everyone from the child experiencing challenges to parents observing their child's struggles. The social stigma permeates into the medical field as it applies a Band-Aid approach using medications. *Solving the ADHD Riddle* addresses many questions, including why this is happening to my child. It gives explanations with stories that make you laugh and cry as they resonate with your own experience as a parent. Most importantly, this book offers an alternative view along with a noninvasive treatment other than medications."

—Robert Nunez, parent

"Dr. McReynolds has made significant contributions to neuroscience and education, especially for children with ADHD. Her research shows significant improvement results with both children and adults. It provides clarity and hope for resolving challenging learning problems using neurofeedback sessions coupled with accurate diagnosis of auditory and visual learning problems. This treatment will benefit many teachers, children, and their families to overcome their learning disabilities and succeed in school and life. This highly readable book is thorough and revolutionary. *Solving the ADHD Riddle* provides new solutions to a problem that impacts both children and adults, bringing hope, relief, and lasting results!"

—Dr. Lila Wills Bronson,
educational consultant and administrative coach

"I cannot say enough wonderful things about the staff and work of Dr. McReynolds. I have recommended neurofeedback to many of my colleagues and friends who have children with special needs and other concerns. Dr. McReynolds and all of her clinicians encouraged, supported, and helped my youngest daughter with her brain development."

—Dana, mother

"My son was diagnosed with ADD, and the only treatment his pediatrician offered was ADD medicine. We contacted Dr. McReynolds in hope to find another alternative. His change is really amazing. He is now able to focus at school."

—Serena, mother

"The change in my son is so impressive. He tried to pass his written driver's license test 6 times prior to neurofeedback. He said it helped him focus and concentrate to pass the exam. I will be forever grateful to Dr. McReynolds."

—Cesar, father

SOLVING

THE

ADHD
RIDDLE

SOLVING
—THE—
ADHD
RIDDLE

The Real Cause and Lasting Solutions
to Your Child's Struggle to Learn

Connie McReynolds, Ph.D.

Published by Educational Insights Press, 1901 Orange Tree Lane, Redlands, California, U.S.A.

Visit the author's website at www.conniemcreynolds.com

The names and some identifying characteristics of the individuals presented in this book have been changed to protect their privacy. Any resulting resemblance to persons living or dead is entirely coincidental and unintentional.

Limit of Liability/Disclaimer of Warranty: The information presented in this book is not meant to substitute for the advice of your physician, your child's pediatrician, or other trained healthcare professionals. You are advised to consult with healthcare professionals with regard to all matters that may require medical attention or diagnosis and to check with a physician before administering or undertaking any course of treatment. Although the publisher and the author have made every effort to ensure that the information in this book was correct at press time and while this publication is designed to provide accurate information in regard to the subject matter covered, the publisher and the author assume no responsibility for errors, inaccuracies, omissions, or any other inconsistencies herein and hereby disclaim any liability to any party for any loss, damage, or disruption caused by errors or omissions, whether such errors or omissions result from negligence, accident, or any other cause.

Chapter 12 Coauthor: Cynthia Britt
Editors: Melanie Votaw and Beacon Point
Proofreading: Michele Wojciechowski
Cover design: BigPoints/99designs
Author photograph: Ishaan Reyna
Publishing Consultant: Geoff Affleck, authorpreneurbooks.com

ISBN: 979-8-9880759-0-5 (paperback)
ISBN: 979-8-9880759-1-2 (ebook)
ISBN: 979-8-9880759-2-9 (audiobook)
Library of Congress Number: 2023902848

Publisher's Cataloging-in-Publication data

Name: McReynolds, Connie, author.
Title: Solving the ADHD riddle : the real cause and lasting solutions to your child's struggle to learn / Connie McReynolds, Ph.D.
Description: Includes bibliographical references. | Redlands, CA: Educational Insights Press, 2023.
Subjects: LCSH Attention-deficit hyperactivity disorder--Treatment. | Attention-deficit-disordered children--United States. | Hyperactive children--United States. | Neurofeedback. | BISAC FAMILY & RELATIONSHIPS / Attention Deficit Disorder (ADD-ADHD) | FAMILY & RELATIONSHIPS / Children with Special Needs | FAMILY & RELATIONSHIPS / Education | FAMILY & RELATIONSHIPS / Learning Disabilities | PSYCHOLOGY / Psychopathology / Attention-Deficit Disorder (ADD-ADHD)
Classification: LCC RJ506.H9 .M 2023 | DDC 618.928589--dc23

*To all the parents who are looking
for an alternative way to help their children
who are struggling to learn.*

"You cannot solve a problem from the same consciousness that created it. You must learn to see the world anew."

—Albert Einstein

TABLE OF CONTENTS

INTRODUCTION

Many books have been written on ADHD, but few, if any, identify the cause of the problem as a *solvable* condition. One of my goals in writing this book is to help parents and teachers understand the differences between a traditional view of ADHD and the one I have come to understand over 13 years of working with children in my clinics.

As a licensed psychologist and professor for more than 25 years, as a rehabilitation counseling professional for more than 30 years, and with more than a decade of clinical results using neurofeedback, I have uncovered what I believe to be the *real* cause of ADHD and found effective solutions that do not involve stimulant medications.

The real cause of ADHD is rooted in auditory and visual processing problems that affect a child's ability to concentrate, focus, remember, be organized, and follow through. By uncovering the actual *cause* of the behavior, I get to the core of the problem. Children in my clinics have gone from failing in school to being on the honor roll.

My desire to find a solution to seemingly unsolvable learning problems and to dive deeper into helping those with ADHD stemmed from my mother. She was a second-grade teacher who was always looking for ways to help students who had trouble learning. My mother taught second grade for 32 years in the same classroom, and I learned the ways of teaching from her and other family members. In particular, I remember one little boy, Danny, who couldn't learn to read. My mother was so concerned about him that over the summer, she drove him 90 miles round-trip to and from the university for special reading assistance. I was always in tow for these trips, which we made regularly throughout that summer.

The professors at the university teaching center ran some assessments and determined that Danny had something called dyslexia, which wasn't well understood or diagnosed in the late 1960s. My mother was so grateful to the teaching center for identifying his problem and for the suggestions of how to teach him so that he could learn to read. Danny went on to do well in school and graduated from high school. That experience has stayed with me all these years as I recall how my mother felt when she found the answers to help little Danny.

Fast forward through my many years as a professor and clinical director to today, when I have found a lasting solution to help parents solve the confusing riddle of ADHD.

As many parents of children with ADHD know, it can be a challenging journey to find a workable solution to the problems their child experiences. There are hundreds of books on the subject, but parents still find themselves struggling to help their children. ADHD has been described in ways ranging from the scary-sounding label of "neurodevelopmental disorder," implying a serious brain problem, to other descriptors that call the child bored, restless, disorganized, unable to pay attention, unable to follow through, tending to drift off, or forgetful. These behaviors take on new meaning when we understand that they're auditory and visual processing problems. The behaviors then become a language to be decoded.

The behaviors of children with ADHD are commonly misunderstood. We tend to view behavior based on what we *think* it means. For instance, if we believe a child is being disrespectful, we view the behavior as disrespectful. If we believe the behavior is willful, we see the behavior as intentional. If we see a child as needing help, we respond by providing or seeking help. When problematic behaviors are seen as a type of communication, this change leads to more compassion about why the unwanted behaviors are occurring. This book will help you understand this point of view.

It will provide valuable information about:

- how the brain learns
- the significance of auditory and visual processing problems
- how these processing problems impact school and behavioral interventions
- practical tips for parents and teachers to support learning
- why punishment doesn't result in lasting changes for children with attention problems
- why neurofeedback is a safe alternative therapy for attention, concentration, and memory problems

Informed by specific assessment results about their child, parents are often tearful and relieved when they learn they don't have a "bad" child. Instead, they have a child who needs help to be able to learn. This is where my clinical intervention of neurofeedback—a process of retraining the brain to improve its functioning—helps resolve the problems they have been experiencing, sometimes for years. This is where hope enters the room and success is created.

This book tells the story of what I have learned that affects so many children and their ability to learn: how to do math, read, spell, behave, and thrive. I will share multiple stories of children I have worked with over the past decade. Through their stories, you'll see how your child's life and your family's life can change for the better once the true cause of their behaviors is identified and resolved.

The information on these pages is for parents who are looking for a better way to help their child who's struggling to learn, for parents of children whose behaviors aren't getting better from restrictions or punishments, and for parents who are hoping to find a way to avoid medications to address their child's ADHD symptoms. It will help parents, educators, and professionals support children like the ones whose stories are included here.

If you would like to learn more or have questions about your unique situation, you're welcome to contact me directly. I'm happy to help. Here's to helping your child thrive.

CHAPTER 1

THE RIDDLE OF ADHD

L iving within the riddle of ADHD can be a frustrating and confusing journey for parents and children who are seeking a lasting
solution. Most of the information about ADHD has focused on
traditional views requiring medications, behavioral interventions,
or a combination of the two, with the belief that ADHD cannot be
resolved.

The information I will share with you, which is based on more
than a decade of helping children resolve these problems, provides a
different interpretation of what is contributing to your child's learning,
attention, memory, concentration, and organizational challenges. To
understand what's causing behaviors that are linked to ADHD, you
have to understand what is happening in the brains of children with
ADHD.

Why is it So Hard?

You may have tried to understand what's going on in your child's brain,
but only come up with more questions. Over more than a decade of
working with children diagnosed with ADHD and other disorders, I
have seen parents struggle to understand why it's so difficult to parent
their child. They're concerned they may not be parenting well enough,
and they see the pain in their child's eyes when frustrations run high
and words hurt.

Parents and children can both feel like they're failing, yet no one seems to have answers. Emotions erupt, but nothing changes. Some question why their child's school isn't doing more to help, or why the interventions don't seem to make a lasting difference. Some push for better results by requesting more or different types of interventions, and some push their child for better behavior and grades without lasting changes.

When interventions don't lead to improvements, some parents look for answers in assessments from doctors, pediatricians, psychologists (school or outside), counselors, and social workers. Children are given psychoeducational assessments, neuropsychological assessments, and medical assessments, or even undergo brain mapping to try to find an answer. Although these can provide answers and lead to effective interventions for some, the answers all too often remain unsatisfying and unclear.

Some parents say they just want their child to "wake up," "pay attention," and "get with it." Sometimes, it seems like their child is aware, but other times, they aren't. They feel confused and puzzled by their child's behaviors. Some families opt for medications, hoping for a cure, while others do so reluctantly because they're pressured to do *something* about their child. Behind each of these approaches is a common worry that their child may fail in school and ultimately in life. Most parents will do whatever they can to keep this from happening.

One little boy I knew had been expelled from multiple kindergarten settings for his unruly behaviors. His parents and grandparents were at a loss about what to do. Another family had trouble getting proper support from the school for their son. The teacher believed his attention would improve if he was made to sit on a one-legged stool!

I've worked with hundreds of such families who have struggled with the riddle of ADHD. Together, we have witnessed the transformative power of treating the root cause of their child's problematic behaviors.

This process often begins with a sense that *something* is wrong, but with a great deal of uncertainty about *what* is wrong and, more importantly, what can be done about it. That was the case for Abigail and her grandmother, and many of the other families you'll meet in this book.

Abigail: Distracted, Disruptive, Determined

I first met Abigail, a seven-year-old force of nature, at a presentation she attended with her grandmother. I was speaking about our new program that helps children and adults train their brains for enhanced focus, attention, and memory. It was my second presentation of the day, and the room was filled to capacity.

The children and adults were excited to try their abilities to run a computer game with their brain. Time was limited, as several children had already tried it. I noticed that one little girl had positioned herself in the front row by her own choice, as her grandmother was seated in the back of the room. She had been fully engaged in my presentation and watching the other children operate the video games with a wireless headset.

As I explained to the group, the game works based on sustained attention. When the person is able to maintain attention for a long enough time, the attention bar at the bottom of the screen moves to the right. With consistency, the barrel on the computer screen explodes as a visual reward for doing well. I could see this little girl wanted to play the game, so I allowed her to give it a try even though we were nearly out of time. This time, though, the computer didn't respond as it had with the other children.

I usually allow each person a few minutes to try playing the game, but since Abigail seemed so determined, I let her continue longer. Even with the additional tries, however, she couldn't make the program work. I suggested we try a different program, but she would have none of it, emphatically saying, "No, I want to do this! I know I can do this!" She said it with surprising command and determination for a seven-year-old. After a few more minutes, she figured it out.

Sparks began to fly from the barrel until she blew it up using her brain waves. Everyone in the room cheered her success.

It was several months later when I saw this little girl again—this time at my clinic. Abigail was accompanied by her grandmother, her legal custodian since age three-and-a-half. During the intake, Abigail sat quietly in her chair and, in a very soft voice, shared that her mother used to hurt her. Later on, when she was out of the room taking the computer assessment, her grandmother said it had been tough for Abigail. She'd been raised in a drug environment, had a family history of ADHD, and had been physically abused by her mother because of her "bad" behavior.

Abigail was diagnosed with ADHD and oppositional defiant disorder (ODD). She was always fidgeting, unable to sit still, and she easily became frustrated and angry. She acted out in the classroom and was often in trouble for poor behavior. She was unable to focus in school, do her homework, or complete simple tasks such as getting ready for school in the morning. In her kindergarten class, she often swung like a monkey from the whiteboard, didn't pay attention, couldn't follow along, and was a constant distraction. In fact, she was so disruptive that her kindergarten teacher told Abigail she was going to quit teaching because of her.

The medications she was prescribed for ADHD helped at school, but when they wore off later at home, she was easily agitated and had meltdowns that her grandmother described as "cataclysmic"—an especially frustrating predicament since she also described Abigail as an "incredible child." Whenever Abigail was learning something, she would ask how to do it, figure it out, and then figure out how to do it better.

It was a difficult story to hear, as this child had seemed so precocious when I met her months earlier and had no awareness of her backstory. She'd been through so much, yet it was encouraging to see that her spirit was so bright. She had great potential for a wonderful future. If her difficulties could be identified and addressed, she might have a chance to make use of her sharp intellect and strong determination.

As you'll read in a later chapter, Abigail experienced remarkable results from neurofeedback that changed her life for the better in dramatic ways.

Antonio: In a Tunnel with No Light

Antonio was seven when he was diagnosed with clinical depression and later, ADHD. Although he tested high on school assessments, his grades were poor because he couldn't focus. He struggled with anger management and self-control, which affected his grades, causing him to fail math class. He later said it was like being in a tunnel with no light at the end.

Antonio had been in special education classes since elementary school. By high school, he was an angry teenager bent on destruction, often fighting with other students. One day, he made a choice that landed him in a lot of trouble. He was bored and had a knack for computers, so he decided to hack the school's computer database system (remember, he had been in special education since elementary school!). After he was expelled from school for this incident, he felt suicidal.

His father was at his wit's end. Deeply concerned for his son's health and well-being, he reached out to see whether we could help. When they came to the clinic the first time, Antonio seemed uninterested in being there. In fact, it seemed like he would rather be just about anywhere else. He barely answered questions and made limited eye contact. Still, he was willing to take the computer-based assessment, so we could learn more about how his brain processed information.

Antonio's assessment revealed he had problems in specific areas of auditory and visual processing that included auditory focus, auditory consistency, and visual comprehension (see Appendix E for his assessment report). These problems weren't about his vision or his hearing. They were about his inability to process certain aspects of auditory and visual information. The findings suggested he had trouble listening consistently and following what people said to him, which meant he was missing important information and feeling frustrated when he didn't know what to do.

Antonio also had problems with combined sustained attention, which meant he had difficulty paying attention over time when someone spoke to him or showed him how to do a task (elements of both auditory and visual processing). This meant he was likely to periodically "tune out" in the classroom unless he was actively engaged. In addition, he had significant problems when under pressure, such as taking a test. Because of these challenges, he needed information presented at a slower pace so his brain could keep up. His scores also revealed that he was likely to become bored and that his mind was likely to wander, which led to unusual or off-task responses (remember, he was bored when he hacked the computer). In all, the combination of limitations across both auditory and visual processing areas contributed to his unwanted or "bad" behaviors.

Following neurofeedback therapy, Antonio transferred to a new school, succeeded in his academic work, was able to keep up with the pace of classroom instructions, and went on to attend college. He later shared with me that if he hadn't gone through neurofeedback, he likely would have hurt himself or someone else.

What do Abigail and Antonio have in common? Both had ADHD. Both had behavioral problems, and both were struggling to manage themselves. Both were considered "problems" at school, yet both were very intelligent. And most importantly, both had *unidentified* auditory and visual processing problems that led to behavioral problems.

When a child has difficulties remembering, following through, listening, or paying attention, the child probably has auditory or visual processing problems. As we'll explore in the next chapter, this is the cause of many of the confusing challenges of children with ADHD.

CHAPTER 2

UNDERSTANDING THE REAL CAUSE

In order for your child to be able to thrive in a learning environment, their brain must be able to pay attention. In order for them to pay attention, their brain has to be able to *process* information—to hold on to the information long enough to store it in their memory bank. Effective processing (storing) is necessary for your child to follow through on tasks, do homework, pick up their toys, make the bed, remember to brush their teeth, get ready for school, and remember where they put their backpack or homework.

Processing and paying attention are intertwined, and both are necessary to function and thrive in the world. When a child can't process or pay attention, they have difficulties that can lead to problematic behaviors. The inability to effectively process information is why a child can do some tasks, yet fail at others. When brain processing is inconsistent, a child will be inconsistent in their ability to perform.

Attention, Processing, and Memory: The Elements of Learning and Recall

Brain processing, memory, learning, and perception are all linked to attention.[1] Your child's brain must be able to hang on to information in order to accurately interpret instructions and complete tasks.

To better understand the term "processing" as it's used here, let's use the analogy of a computer. In order for the computer to do what you want, it has to be able to run programs or "process" your commands. Your child's brain also has to be able to run the programs (remembering and sequencing tasks) in order to do what's asked (results). When their brain is unable to remember and sequence what was said (process), the child is unable to consistently follow through.

Children who are unable to pay attention are unable to respond appropriately because paying attention is directly related to how well their brain processes information. In other words, attention is the foundation of how they learn. Without attention, a child is unable to focus consistently and absorb what they're taught.

As Donald A. Norman described in his book *Memory & Attention*:

"Limited processing . . . invariably implies a competition for attention . . . The term *inattention* . . . implies that, at a given moment, the thing being attended to is either not what it was intended to be or not what adaptively it ought to be. If a single definition could be derived . . . it would refer . . . to the state of the individual through which learning takes place. [Attention] makes heavy demands upon the brain's processing capacity."[2]

The opposite is inattentiveness, which causes people to be distracted, drift off, and miss out on important details. For example, consider driving down the freeway and realizing you have missed your exit. This has happened to most of us at some point and is a great example of a lack of attention when we aren't present in the moment and become distracted. Imagine this happening throughout your day, which is what inattentiveness is like for children.

It's important to mention, however, that brain processing problems aren't the same as cognitive delays, developmental delays, or intellectual limitations. These terms are often confused with symptoms seen in children who have auditory and visual processing problems, especially in school settings. In my opinion, thousands of children may be misidentified as needing special education services, when the cause of their learning problems may actually be due to weaknesses in auditory and visual processing. Processing problems aren't about intelligence, but children with processing problems can appear to have developmental or cognitive delays.

Most children with ADHD symptoms are unable to self-regulate, follow through, pay attention, or do what's asked of them because of weak auditory and visual processing abilities. A child has to be able to understand and remember information, which requires attention and memory.[3]

And attention and memory are related to auditory and visual processing. When attention and memory aren't working, implementing interventions is challenging, as the intervention will require the child to pay attention and remember the instructions in order to follow through. This becomes a no-win situation for children who have attention and memory problems associated with auditory and visual processing.

Auditory and Visual Processing Problems

Auditory and visual processing problems aren't about your child's physical ability to hear or see. They're about the brain's ability to work with verbal and visual information and how it holds on to and manages information.

Simply put, auditory and visual processing problems interfere with a child's ability to learn, causing memory difficulties, concentration problems, lack of focus, inability to follow instructions, disorganization, anger and frustration, outbursts and temper tantrums, and low self-confidence. Many of these symptoms are associated with ADHD. However, I have found they can also be the direct result of auditory and visual processing problems, which is one of the reasons ADHD medications don't work for some children. The medications don't treat the root cause of these problems.

Many of the identified symptoms of ADD, ADHD, anxiety, depression, learning problems, memory, focus, and attention can be improved by strengthening a child's auditory and visual processing. When auditory and visual processing problems are identified and resolved, the behavioral, emotional, and learning problems go away or are much less challenging. Brain processes are strengthened, children experience positive life changes, and they may be able to reduce or eliminate the need for some medications.

In particular, auditory and visual processing problems play a direct role in a child's ability to learn to read. The data speak volumes. For example, if a child hasn't learned to read at grade level by the end of third grade, that child is four times less likely to graduate from high school by age 19 than the child who's reading proficiently at the end of third grade.[4,5] And it is significantly higher than rates seen in children with basic reading skills (9 percent) or those who are proficient readers (4 percent).[6]

This is because through third grade, which is a pivotal point in education, children are learning to read. From fourth grade on, children are reading to learn. For a child who struggles with reading, learning becomes much more difficult.[7] Limited reading ability leads to chronic absences, poor behavior, and failing in math or language arts by the time a child is in sixth grade.[8,9]

High school dropouts are at greater risk of becoming involved in the criminal justice system, with nearly one in ten young male high school dropouts ending up in jail or juvenile detention. The cost of just one high school dropout serving time in jail or prison is nearly $300,000.[10] Therefore, reading at grade level by the end of third grade is an important milestone, making it all the more important for the early identification of auditory and visual processing problems since that type of processing is critical when learning to read.

Types of Behaviors: Inconsistency, Inattention, and Escalation

Children with auditory and visual processing problems often daydream, appear disorganized, have difficulty following through, seem not to listen, or seem to be somewhere else. These are the children who are forgetful, frequently losing things, are easily distracted, can't maintain focus, or act out. Parents will ask their child to do something and believe they "have it," only to be disappointed yet again with a lack of follow-through. Parents have been heard to say, "We just talked about this, and you agreed. What happened?" or may ask, "Why do I always have to remind you to do something?" These are all typical descriptions of children with ADHD.[11] But this is the riddle of processing problems—sometimes they remember and sometimes they don't.

Children with these types of problems are described as smart, yet they're inconsistent. When this happens repeatedly, everyone begins to feel discouraged and frustrated. Depending on the level of unwanted or troubling behaviors, some parents begin to feel irritated or angry with their child, thinking the behavior is on purpose. Emotions can lead to outbursts, with some parents thinking that doing something—anything—to get their child's attention will help.

Some parents use punishments, thinking the negative consequences will improve attention and follow-through. However, as many parents and teachers have found, nothing seems to make a difference. Punishments and restrictions fail because the unwanted behaviors are most likely beyond the child's control. Ultimately, this is a child who doesn't understand why they're getting into trouble. When asked why they did _____ (fill in the blank), they have trouble answering. It's beyond their awareness because they have no other experience or frame of reference.

In many instances, children with auditory and visual processing problems can accomplish certain activities very well. For example, they may be good at sports and especially good at playing video games.

These activities don't require the same type of brain processing skills that schoolwork requires. They may be able to sit for hours playing video games, yet unable to focus for ten minutes to finish a homework assignment. For many parents, this inconsistency is both confusing and frustrating. The confusion is compounded when a child can sometimes accomplish what's asked of them, but not always. This only makes it appear more so to be willful "bad" behavior.

For example, you may tell or show your child how to do a homework assignment, but they're unable to complete it even though you explained it. Put yourself in their shoes. If you (as an adult) can't remember the instructions that someone told you, it will be difficult to complete the task. The struggle is the difference between what you want to do (follow through) and what you're unable to do (can't remember the instructions). This is the discrepancy you're seeing in your child.

Processing problems can affect many aspects of your child's ability to change their behaviors. For example, if they're experiencing auditory processing problems, they might not be able to remember what was said or follow instructions. If they have visual processing problems, they might not be able to organize their backpack or remember where they put something.

When they don't remember, adults often assume they're distracted, forgetful, inattentive, disorganized, or have poor memory. All of these are technically true. But children with these processing problems aren't choosing to be disorganized or forgetful. In other words, your child isn't deliberately trying to upset you, disobey you, or do bad things. If auditory and visual processing problems are present, they simply may not be able to pay attention (attend and remember) long enough to follow through or change their behavior.

Children with auditory and visual processing problems don't understand why they struggle and can't do the same school assignments as their peers. At the same time, teachers and parents are at a loss. After all, if you're unaware of processing problems, how can you explain why you didn't finish a task, assignment, or project? This is where the majority of problems occur for children who have attention problems, and this is the difference we will continue to explore throughout the book.

CHAPTER 3

MISUNDERSTANDING THE PROBLEM

The behaviors of children with attention and learning problems are commonly misunderstood. This is based in attribution theory, which means that what we believe about a behavior affects how we think and react to the behavior and can vary from person to person.

Since behaviors hold the meanings we give them, there are many interpretations of them. Psychiatrists see mental dysfunction and prescribe medications. Behaviorists see behavioral problems and implement behavioral interventions. Parents see bad behavior and implement punishment. A teacher who feels disrespected may dismiss the child from the classroom, while some schools will expel the child. Others see a child in need and provide support.

To uncover the reason for these behaviors, we need to decode their meaning. In doing so, it may be possible to find a true solution.

Behaviors are Communication

It's difficult for children to explain or describe the trouble they're having or the reasons for their behaviors. Instead, they may demonstrate their difficulties through their behaviors.[1] The problem comes when the behaviors are seen *as* the problem. Parents and teachers want to reduce or eliminate the unwanted behaviors as quickly as possible, but before that, they need to decode the behaviors to understand their meaning. What are the behaviors telling them?

When properly decoded, behaviors are a type of language children use to tell adults what they're going through. And when problematic behaviors are seen as a form of communication to be decoded, we have greater compassion for the child. So, to open the door to alternative ways of resolving the problems, we must shift from focusing on eliminating them to seeking to understand what the child is communicating through them.

Obviously, an intervention that identifies and corrects the underlying cause of the behaviors is more likely to result in lasting changes than an intervention that doesn't. So this shift in thinking has the potential to create positive benefits for all involved—you, your child, and your child's teacher.

The behaviors of children with auditory and visual processing problems can look like other medical or psychological problems. This puzzling situation has led to many diagnostic labels, some of which may not be correct, such as the following that were given to children seen in my clinics:

- attention deficit disorder (ADD)
- attention deficit/hyperactivity disorder (ADHD)
- oppositional defiant disorder (ODD)
- intermittent explosive disorder (IED)
- anger management problems
- cognitive/developmental/intellectual delays
- tics
- Tourette's syndrome
- autistic-like behaviors
- processing problems
- sensory problems

- learning disorders (LD)
- slow learner
- executive functioning impairment

Some medical conditions also mimic the symptoms of ADHD, such as sleep problems, substance abuse, mood disorders, hearing or vision problems, learning disabilities, sensory processing disorders, giftedness, seizure disorder, obsessive-compulsive disorder, Tourette's syndrome, and autism spectrum disorder.[2] Although it's important to rule out these conditions or treat them if they do exist, some children diagnosed with one or more of them were later found to have auditory and visual processing problems that could be successfully treated.

If your child has auditory and visual processing problems, but has been diagnosed with another condition, the recommended treatment may be focused on solving the wrong problem. Although a diagnostic label can provide insight, if that label is incorrect, your child is unlikely to benefit from the interventions.

Typical ADHD Interventions

Physicians, psychiatrists, psychologists, social workers, and school counselors typically recommend medications or behavioral interventions with the intent of reducing or eliminating undesirable behaviors. Yet, parents in my clinics have reported that typical interventions haven't brought about lasting improvements for their children. These parents have complained of continued inappropriate behaviors, low grades, trouble with peer relationships, memory problems, and medication side effects.

Finding appropriate treatments is vital since children who experience symptoms of ADHD tend to be at greater risk of poorer outcomes such as lower academic attainment, impaired social functioning, increased risk of hospital admissions, increased substance use, and reduced employability as adults.[3-9]

Some child experts have expressed concerns about the overuse of the ADHD diagnosis.[10] Case in point—about 11 percent of school-aged children in the United States or 6.4 million children were diagnosed with ADHD from 2003 to 2012, which was a 42 percent increase over the previous reporting period.[11] In 2018, about 6.1 million U.S. children had an ADHD diagnosis, nearly 62 percent were prescribed medication, and about 47 percent received behavioral treatment.[12]

As many parents know, traditional treatment for ADHD encompasses either behavior modification, medication, or both. The results of these individual or dual interventions have positive outcomes for some children[13] but not for others.[14]

Several studies identify concerns associated with some medications and behavioral interventions. Because research about side effects and the lack of long-term results may not be readily available to parents, the following sections will give you a brief overview.

Bear in mind that this information isn't intended to imply medications or behavioral interventions won't work for your child. They're simply meant to highlight some concerns that you may want to consider as a parent. You need to be informed in order to make the best decision for your child and, as appropriate, in consultation with your treating physician.

Behavioral Interventions

School-based behavioral interventions are designed to support students who are struggling in the general education setting. They use a reward approach with the intent of promoting positive behaviors and eliminating negative behaviors. But an in-depth review of these approaches didn't find substantial positive, long-term treatment effects for ADHD.[15,16] And while some ADHD behavioral interventions were associated with positive benefits, which included empowering parents and reducing the conduct problems of children, there were no positive results for academic and social skills.[17]

As I've said, interventions that require auditory and visual processing abilities may have limited effectiveness when a child is unable to remember what they've been shown or told to do. This doesn't necessarily mean the intervention is ineffective, but it simply won't work well for a child with these challenges.

Medication Interventions

When it comes to medication, various studies suggest concerns that you may want to consider. This isn't an exhaustive listing, nor is the information in this chapter intended as medical advice. I provide it here, however, to help you work better in concert with your child's treating physician to determine the most appropriate intervention.

- Bone loss (i.e., osteopenia) was found in children who were taking methylphenidate (Ritalin), dexmethylphenidate (Focalin), dextroamphetamine (Dexedrine), atomoxetine (Strattera), and lisdexamfetamine (Vyvanse) medications.
    - Almost 25 percent of the children in the study had lower bone-mineral density in the femur, femoral neck, and lumbar spine compared with children who hadn't taken any of these medications.
    - Researchers note that the side effects of gastrointestinal problems lead to decreased appetite and an upset stomach, which could worsen nutrition and diminish calcium intake.[18]
- The use of methylphenidate (Ritalin, Concerta, Medikinet, Equasym) resulted in a 60 percent higher risk of sleep problems and nearly 300 percent greater risk of decreased appetite.[19]
- Height suppression of 1 to 1.5 inches was associated with the long-term use of ADHD medication.[20]

- Physical growth (height and weight) was diminished in children following 14 months of intensive medication treatment.[21]

- A long-term follow-up study[22] found evidence of height suppression in young adults after consistent use of medication from childhood to adulthood.

- Medication didn't have long-lasting effects, with fewer than 50 percent of the children in the study remaining consistent with their dosage over a six-month period.[23]

- Fewer than 10 percent of ADHD cases used medication consistently from childhood to adulthood, and long-term use wasn't found to reduce symptom severity in adulthood. Even with ADHD medications, some children showed little or no improvement in their behaviors.[24,25]

- Despite initial indications of a long-term benefit over the first two years, additional analyses after three treatment years didn't show any long-term relative advantages of ongoing treatment with stimulants.[26]

- A review and meta-data analysis of 43 studies involving 2,110 children revealed that drug treatment benefited a child's school performance by 15 percent at most, and a maximum of only 14 percent of children were viewed as more on-task.[27]

- Nearly 90 percent of the 186 children investigated in a particular study continued to struggle with ADHD symptoms after six years of drug treatment for ADHD, and long-term use of the medications didn't reduce their symptoms. Instead, the children were found to have symptoms as severe as those who never took medications for ADHD.[28]

- Children as young as preschool age are being prescribed medications,[29] but some professionals conclude that the use of stimulants is too simple of an approach for the complex factors that cause the behavioral and emotional difficulties.[30]

- The limited benefits of stimulant medication are an important reason to consider alternative therapies.[31]

The Wrong Treatment for the Wrong Problem

So why do ADHD symptoms seem to persist for some children following traditional treatment approaches? ADHD medications weren't developed for, and may not be suited for, auditory and visual processing difficulties. They were primarily developed to reduce observable behavioral symptoms, such as restlessness, inattentiveness, lack of focus, and hyperactivity.

For children with auditory and visual processing difficulties, the long-term resolution of behavioral problems may not be achieved with medication. Behavioral interventions, meanwhile, may overlook the auditory and visual processing problems.

These children need a different long-term solution for their behavioral and learning problems. Again, this means identifying the real meaning of the problems and treating their root cause.

CHAPTER 4

IDENTIFYING AND TREATING THE ROOT CAUSE

When children are unable to do what's asked, cannot organize school-work, or are unable to follow through with repeated instructions, they may be diagnosed with ADHD, which has become a catch-all for many behavioral, attention, and learning problems. Again, children with auditory or visual processing problems have behaviors commonly identified with ADHD, and they're often diagnosed based on their behaviors.

Yet, in more than 13 years of working with children and adults, I have encountered only one woman who could describe her experience of auditory and visual processing problems. Most people, whether an adult or child, can't explain the problem so that others understand it. They feel overwhelmed by the sense that their life isn't working well and don't understand why people get frustrated with them.

Children aren't failing because they want to, nor are they failing because they're lazy or not trying. They want to succeed and make people happy. In fact, it's often what they want more than anything. But they simply can't. They feel worried and scared that they're going to get in trouble yet again. So auditory and visual processing difficulties cause considerable emotional and psychological stress.

These negative feelings can lead to behavioral problems, withdrawing, or shutting down. Even though they may be trying hard, adults will tell them to try harder. Over the years, I have heard parents ask:

- Why won't she try?
- Why is homework always such a battle?
- How can he fail his spelling test when he knew the words on the way to school?
- Am I a bad parent?
- Is the school failing?
- Why can't he learn?
- How is she ever going to make it in the world?
- How will he get through high school or go to college?
- Do I just have a "bad" child?

Some children act out while others withdraw—but neither response brings relief. Instead, they often encounter more defeat, punishment, shaming, negative comments, or even bullying. It feels like a no-win situation with no way out.

Unidentified attention and processing problems also often look different between boys and girls. For example, boys may be restless or act like the class clown,[1] which can help disguise fears of rejection caused by difficulties with learning. Negative acting-out behavior can disguise problems with following along, comprehending instructions, and focus.

Rather than act out, girls tend to hide or withdraw in a classroom. They don't want to draw attention to themselves and their problems. As a result, their attention and processing problems aren't identified as frequently as boys. Girls are often passed on to the next grade in school even when they're progressively falling behind in their academic work. In the end, girls may fare worse due to their auditory and visual processing problems. For example, girls with processing problems have an increased incidence of attempted suicide and other forms of self-injurious behaviors.[2,3] In addition, due to a lack of success in school, they are nine times more likely to become single mothers than their peers who go on to earn a college degree.[4]

Regardless of gender, all children who struggle in school due to auditory and visual processing problems are at risk of a negative path that includes a decreased likelihood of completing high school, a higher incidence of involvement with the criminal justice system, and diminished employment outcomes.[5-9]

The Lived Experience of Processing Problems

To better understand what a child experiences with processing problems, let's take a walk in their shoes. For the moment, imagine you're in a familiar place and know the people around you. While you trust them, they seem to get upset with you a lot, and you don't know why. They keep saying things, yet you can't remember what they say. So nothing makes sense.

You have learned that to get along and not cause trouble, you *act* like you understand. You've learned not to ask questions because asking has caused problems in the past. You've been accused of not paying attention and told you don't listen. But you don't understand what this means. You suspect you aren't very smart because you get in trouble no matter how hard you try.

You've started to tell yourself that there must be something wrong with you because when you look at others around you, they seem to know what to do. As a result, you feel defeated. You don't know how to respond anymore, so you find it's better to be quiet and just try not to get into trouble. Most of the time, you feel overwhelmed and just want to be left alone. And sometimes you feel frustrated and angry because you can't do what they want you to do even though you're trying your best.

Again, when a child has weak processing abilities, their brain is simply incapable of bringing together the expected thoughts and reactions.

The Good News

Luckily, there is an answer! Over the past decade, my clinical work has led to a different conclusion about ADHD from the ones typically held. By training the brain using neurofeedback that targets the identified auditory and visual processing weaknesses, it's possible to help your child strengthen these processing abilities.

When I understood how to identify the processing problems and how to use neurofeedback to treat them, it became clear why traditional interventions weren't as successful as hoped. This was an eye-opener for me. Finally, it made sense why some children continued to struggle regardless of the interventions they tried. When parents and educators were better informed about the specific learning needs of the child, frustrations lessened between all parties involved.

Let's dig into how neurofeedback works and why it's an effective solution for processing problems. To start, we'll take a look at how the brain works and what's going on in the minds of children with these challenges.

CHAPTER 5

HOW THE BRAIN WORKS

For decades, the word *healing* was rarely used in connection with the brain in the medical community, as it was with other organ systems. The preponderance of belief was that it wasn't possible to heal the brain, which meant most treatments involved the use of some type of medication to "prop up the failing system."[1] For example, ADHD medications help decrease some symptoms by temporarily changing the chemical balance in the brain. Some ADHD medications help it make more neurotransmitters, while others slow down how quickly it absorbs unused neurotransmitters (called reuptake). The belief is that improving the transmission of brain hormones will help children be less hyperactive and improve their attention. But when the person stops taking the medication, the symptoms often return.

In 1949, Canadian Psychologist Donald Hebb presented the idea of *neuroplasticity*, which means that the brain can change and adapt to new information. (The word *neuro* means brain, and *plasticity* means to change). The brain changes its own structure and functioning in response to activities and mental experiences. It literally changes all the time based on what we think and do. Using imaging scans, scientists have been able to observe this phenomenon throughout a person's life. Even older adults can harness the brain's sophisticated restorative abilities to strengthen their brain-processing skills.[2,3]

Fifty years after Dr. Hebb presented the idea of neuroplasticity, Dr. Eric Kandel received the Nobel Prize for demonstrating that as learning occurs, the connections among nerve cells increase. He discovered that learning actually "switches on" genes that change our neural brain structure. Over the past 20 years, hundreds of studies have demonstrated that mental activity is not only the product of the brain, but a shaper of it. Because we better understand how our brain works, we now have the ability to influence, program, and change it, harnessing its own abilities to improve its function.

Through imaging scans, we know that brain cells constantly communicate with one another. They form and re-form new connections, which can be directed to change the brain for better functioning. In other words, it can reprogram and restructure itself. So the power to change your life comes from your brain processing.[4,5] The key is to discover which areas function well and which need strengthening. When we're able to do this with children who have processing and attention problems, they can learn how to strengthen their brain processing abilities and improve their quality of life.

Let's look more in depth at the evolving field of neuroscience and the exciting knowledge that has caused us to rethink what we know about how the brain learns.

Training the Brain

Neuroplasticity is the flexibility of the brain to change regardless of a person's age.[6] The brain is trained and physically changed by thinking or doing something repeatedly. This is one of the most heavily researched topics in the field of neuroscience.

Neuroplasticity helps explain why traditional interventions don't work well for some children, particularly those with auditory and visual processing difficulties. These problems interrupt the brain's ability to focus, attend, remember, and follow through. Since learning requires consistent repetition of information in order to "wire in" the new information, it's difficult for children (or anyone) with attention problems to be consistent enough to train their brain. This is one of the main reasons why children with auditory and visual processing problems struggle to learn or remember to follow the rules.

When your brain is able to attend to information and processes that information in an effective manner, your brain becomes *trained* to perform functions without your focused attention. Consider walking into the room or driving a car. Most of the time, you no longer need to think about putting one foot in front of the other to walk. Similarly, you no longer need to think about placing your hands on the steering wheel when you turn a corner, drive down the street, or park. Your brain has been trained to do these functions in a nearly automatic way.

When the brain is unable to sustain attention and focus long enough to be trained, however, it can be difficult to learn a new skill or follow through. If a child can't focus or remember long enough for their brain to develop the pattern, they may have trouble completing tasks, making it harder to develop routines in their daily life.

Over the past 20 years, science has learned a great deal about how to train the brain and how to strengthen brain processing abilities to function better. For example, we've learned how brain changes work and how to harness the brain's ability to improve functioning that leads to improved lives. This knowledge is significant for you and your child.

Briefly, there are two types of plasticity (ability to change) at work in the brain—short-term and long-term. Knowing about these can help you better understand your child's processing difficulties.

Short-term plasticity (memory) refers to a quick up or down adjustment that helps the brain determine the importance of a conversation. An example of this is when you ask your child to do something, and they seem to be listening. Yet, they quickly forget what was said or what to do. This is tied to your child's short-term brain functioning or short-term memory. Even though it seems that the forgetfulness is on purpose, it may not be. When short-term plasticity isn't working well in their brain, they can have trouble remembering what was said long enough to follow through.

Long-term plasticity (memory) lasts anywhere from minutes to hours, days, or years and is the way that memories are created. Long-term memory is needed to remember how to do many tasks in a daily routine. Children need long-term memory to remember to take their backpack to school each day, put away toys, how to spell words, complete math computations, take out the trash each week, or study for a test. Children with long-term memory problems may have trouble remembering what they learned last year, last week, or yesterday.

Long-term memory is what helps the brain learn and remember, and a child has to first be able to pay attention in order for the information to be stored in the brain. If children with auditory and visual processing difficulties can't store the information long enough for the memory to form, they won't remember it.

In order for the longer-term storage to work, your child may need stronger short-term plasticity. When auditory and visual processing problems interfere with their ability to remember information, these processes need to be strengthened.

Wiring in Change

As part of his thinking about neuroplasticity in the mid-20th century, Dr. Donald Hebb introduced the idea that "cells that fire together, wire together."[7] He wrote that "any two cells or systems of cells that are repeatedly active at the same time will tend to become associated, so that activity in one facilitates activity in the other." In other words, repetition of information is how the brain develops memory patterns and recalls the information later. These memory patterns become the automatic brain functions of remembering how to ride a bike years later, drive a car, walk, or any activity we learned how to do. Our brain becomes wired so that it can function automatically. This is considered the core law of how the brain learns and remembers.

When neurons repeatedly fire together, they develop connections. This means that any repeated mental experience leads to structural changes in the brain's neuronal pathways, making the connections stronger.[8] When we practice an activity, the brain develops a pathway that gets stronger every time we repeat the activity. This is why we can learn to ride a bike as a child and still remember how decades later.

In fact, when we think or do something repeatedly, our brain changes its physical structure. This brain-changing process is sometimes called "wiring" or "brain programming."

Neuronal pathways run our brain processing and are the foundation of everything we do. Think of them as the computer programs our brain uses to help us function.[9] These pathways either work effectively or they don't. When they work well, we're able to accomplish our daily tasks. When they don't, as in the case of auditory and visual processing problems, we probably struggle more than others to accomplish daily tasks.

When the neuronal pathways aren't making strong connections, learning can be difficult, if not impossible, for some children. If there's an interference with the brain's ability to remember information, it will be more difficult for the child to "wire" the information in the brain. Luckily, a person's brain has the potential to rewire itself, which means we can improve many kinds of conditions.

Because the brain learns through repetition, the use of brain training programs designed to strengthen weaker areas of brain processing have been found to be effective in retraining and strengthening the brain.[10-12] Based on how the brain is designed to work, it sets up a self-perpetuating cycle of success or failure that's at the core of why we act, live, and feel the way we do. We know if we want to change our life, we can do so by changing (rewiring) the way our brain works.[13]

Neuroplasticity is the reason why neurofeedback works in helping people improve their attention, focus, and memory; reduce anxiety and depression; and reduce or eliminate trauma. We make these brain changes by strengthening our neuronal pathways. The flexibility of the brain creates a neuronal activity feedback loop that we can learn to influence and control through repeated training processes. This is the basis of the neurofeedback interventions that have proven successful for many people in my clinics.[14-16]

Brain Waves and Neurofeedback Games

To gain an understanding of the neurofeedback process, it's helpful to understand brain waves, which are the result of electrical pulses between large numbers of neurons communicating with each other. This occurs constantly.

An electroencephalogram (EEG) can measure the activity of brain waves. Sensors applied to the scalp in specific locations send information to a computer, providing real-time feedback about brain activities, such as focus and attention.

There are five types of human brain waves, which are measured in Hertz (Hz).

Gamma waves (32+ Hz) are the fastest brain waves and are associated with learning and complex problem-solving abilities, peak focus, and expanded consciousness.

Beta waves (14-32 Hz) are fast brain waves associated with alertness, concentration, and cognition. Excessive beta waves have been associated with ADHD, obsessive-compulsive disorder, sleep disorders, learning disorders, anxiety, and depression.

Alpha waves (8-14 Hz) are often associated with relaxation, visualization, and creativity. Excessive amounts have been associated with ADHD, inattention, distractibility, depression, and anxiety.

Theta waves (4-8 Hz) are slower brain waves associated with meditation, intuition, and memory. Excessive theta wave activity has been linked to confusion, slow reaction times, and difficulties with impulse control, daydreaming, and mental inefficiency.

Delta waves (.51-4 Hz) are the slowest brain waves and are associated with some stages of sleep and detached awareness.

HUMAN BRAIN WAVES

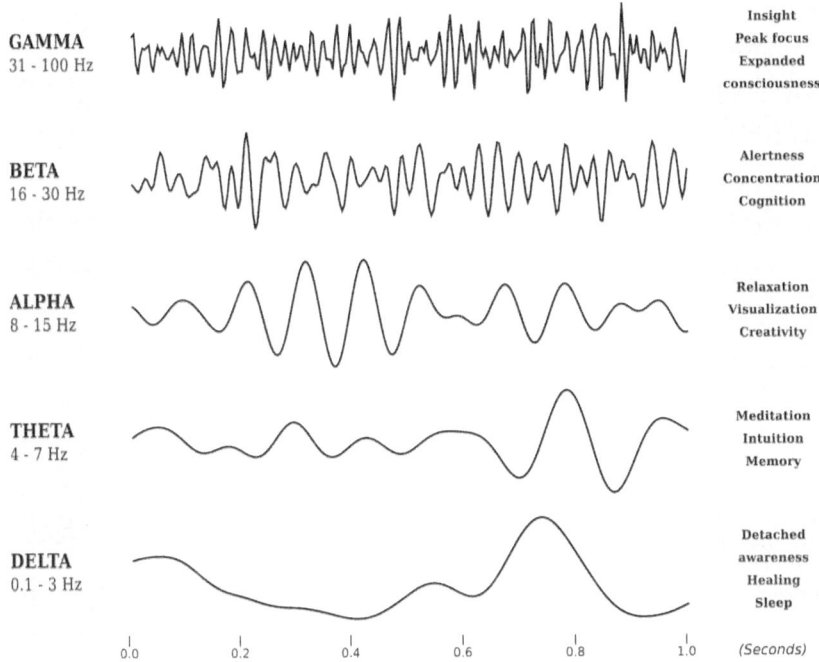

Gamma waves help us process information, so some scientists believe that people with learning difficulties or impaired mental processing may not produce enough of them. Beta brain waves lead to feeling alert and focused, but too much of them can cause anxiety, overthinking, ruminating, obsessive-compulsive disorder, sleep disorders, and learning problems. Alpha waves are the most conducive to learning by helping us maintain focus, but still, too much of them can lead to daydreaming. Theta brain waves are associated with processing information and making memories, but too much of these can cause foggy thinking and slow reaction times, as well as affect judgment and impulse control. Delta brain waves are associated with sleep, but too much of them can lead to learning disorders and difficulty maintaining attention.[17,18]

The neurofeedback process uses the EEG sensors to send brain wave signals to the computer, which uses these signals as a way of providing feedback to the child when playing a training video game. Using the reward system of the video game, the child's brain learns how to produce the required brain state to achieve brain training goals. Through practice, the brain can be trained to create the new habit of improved functioning.

Therefore, through the use of neurofeedback, it's possible to retrain the brain to establish more optimal levels of brain waves that enhance learning, attention, focus, and memory.

Neurotransmitters

Neuronal pathways send signals from one part of the brain to another. These brain processes are orchestrated by the chemical messengers in the brain known as neurotransmitters. Neurotransmitters play an important role in the functioning of your child's brain, and neuronal pathways are what make it possible to do anything from riding a bike to being an astronaut.

I have heard numerous parents remark that their child can play video games for hours but can't focus on homework for ten minutes. There's a reason for this: video games increase certain types of brain hormones (neurotransmitters), while homework does not.

The brain has many neurotransmitter systems that support our ability to function in our lives. As we briefly touch on the brain hormones (neurotransmitters) called acetylcholine, noradrenaline, serotonin, and dopamine, you'll see their importance as they relate to types of video games.

Acetylcholine is involved in regulating emotion, mood, learning, cognitive function, motivation, REM sleep, and short-term memory. It affects our ability to remember information, to learn language, develop relationships, and know what to do.

Noradrenaline (norepinephrine) mobilizes the brain and body for action. It's responsible for our fight or flight response, and it plays an important role in wakefulness, cognitive control, and working memory. **Low levels** can cause difficulty in paying attention, increase depression, and increase hypotension.

Serotonin regulates mood, appetite, impulsivity, social behavior, sleep, and memory. It's called the body's natural feel-good chemical. **Low levels** can cause anxiety, depressed mood, aggression, impulsive behavior, and insomnia. An imbalance of serotonin is associated with generalized anxiety disorder.

Dopamine is involved in motor control, reward and reinforcement, and motivation. It plays a significant role in arousal, aversion, and cognitive control. Dopamine governs attentional control, which is the capacity to choose what to pay attention to and what to ignore. It affects an individual's ability to concentrate and plays a role in significant brain functions:

- *Cognitive inhibition* affects the brain's ability to tune out stimuli irrelevant to the task or process at hand.

- *Inhibitory control* is the ability to inhibit impulses so a person can choose a more appropriate behavior to be able to complete a task.

- *Self-control* is the ability to regulate emotions, thoughts, and behaviors in the face of distractions and impulses.

- *Working memory* helps the brain hold on to information temporarily and helps us reason, make decisions, and regulate behaviors.

- *Cognitive flexibility* is the mental ability to switch between thinking about two different ideas, as well as the ability to think about multiple concepts simultaneously.[19-21]

In children (and adults) with attention problems, dopamine and norepinephrine are often in low supply. Dopamine and serotonin make us feel better while norepinephrine mobilizes the brain for action. When our brain produces these hormones, we feel more alert and capable. When each of these is in short supply, the brain is less alert and focused. Children with attention problems often struggle with homework because it doesn't stimulate their brain's production of these feel-good brain hormones, so their brain is less alert and focused.

Video Games Change the Brain

Video games increase certain types of brain hormones, particularly dopamine. Video gaming has everything to do with brain programming and neuronal pathways. In today's world, parents need to understand how their child's brain may be affected by the various types of games and what to watch for if they have concerns about their child's behaviors.

In 1998, the scientific journal *Nature* published a study[22] that explored the effects of playing video games on the release of the feel-good neurotransmitter dopamine. Researchers discovered that the amount of dopamine released in the brains of children playing video games was similar to the amount seen after an intravenous injection of amphetamine or methylphenidate. In other words, playing video games causes the brain to release large amounts of dopamine—the very neurotransmitter that's often in low supply in the brains of people with attention problems and ADHD.

At first, since their dopamine is in low supply, it may sound like playing these video games and getting that release of dopamine is a good thing. It's difficult, however, to regulate the amount of dopamine being released through playing video games, and overproduction is not a good thing.

The more time a child spends on a rewarding game, the more dopamine is released. The more that's released, the more the child wants to play the rewarding game. This process has the potential to lead to addiction. Based on years of brain research, scientists know that the brain is wired to seek instant gratification and fast-paced activities, which are hallmarks of many video games.

In Neurology Now in 2014, David Greenfield, Ph.D., founder of The Center for Internet and Technology Addiction, said:

"Playing video games floods the pleasure center of the brain with dopamine. That gives gamers a rush—but only temporarily. With all that extra dopamine lurking around, the brain gets the message to produce less of this critical neurotransmitter. The end result: players can end up with a diminished supply of dopamine. Take a game like that away from addicted adolescents [children] and they often show behavioral problems, withdrawal symptoms, even aggression."[23]

As far back as the early 1990s, scientists cautioned that video games stimulate regions of the brain controlling vision and movement. Other parts of the brain that govern behaviors, emotions, and learning can be left behind in a developing brain.[24-26]

Certainly, playing video games could provide benefits such as enhanced visual processing, improved ability to switch between tasks, and improved information processing. These abilities may assist children in developing multitasking skills useful in future school or employment settings. However, these benefits may not outweigh the underdevelopment of necessary skills to succeed in school or keep a job, such as interpersonal behaviors, emotional regulation, and the ability to learn.[27,28]

In particular, certain kinds of video games have been shown to change the brain's processing patterns. Scientific images reflected changes in brain processing between two groups of boys. One group didn't play video games, while the second group played violent video games extensively for two weeks. The video gaming group ended up with lower activity in the brain regions that control behavior as compared to the group that didn't play the violent video games.[29]

The images the scientists saw sent a clear message about the effects of playing video games that involve first-shooter response and other types of violence. The research clearly showed that playing violent video games affects young/adolescent brains in negative ways.

The area of the brain known as the prefrontal cortex—which controls judgment, decision-making, and impulse control—undergoes significant change and reorganization during adolescence. It's also the area of the brain known as the executive functioning control center. Strength in this brain area is necessary to weigh risks and rewards. It also governs the ability to delay gratification, which plays a significant role in decisions like studying for the math exam instead of staying up all night to play video games.

The prefrontal region of the brain isn't fully developed until around age 25. This alone helps explain why children and adolescents can engage in hours of video games while not recognizing the body's need for rest, nutrition, and even proper hygiene.

When the prefrontal region of the brain is underdeveloped, children and adolescents are less able to understand the negative consequences of their behaviors or to control or limit excessive video gaming. A study of 45 adolescents who played violent video games for 30 minutes showed that they experienced lowered activity in the prefrontal regions of the brain.[30-32]

In fact, the dopamine release from video gaming is so powerful that it can almost shut down the prefrontal regions, which is why some children can play these games nonstop for hours. For children with auditory and visual processing problems, playing video games is an attractive distraction from their lives when they're struggling to find success in academic work or life.

Video Gaming Behavioral Side Effects

Action-entertainment video games often attract children with focus, attention, and anger problems, and violent video games reinforce these types of negative behaviors. Playing violent video games for 10-20 minutes has been shown to increase aggressive thoughts in children compared to those who played only nonviolent video games.[33-35]

Children with attention problems, low dopamine, and a desire for instant gratification can't recognize how much time they spend playing video games. Due to these identified potential concerns, you may want to more closely monitor the types of video games and the amount of time your child spends playing even non-violent games. You might need to establish playing time limits and observe if your child shows behavioral changes afterwards. If they do, the following information may be helpful in identifying if your child has a problem.

It may be time to assess the risks of video gaming if your child exhibits the following behaviors. Is your child:

- spending excessive amounts of time on the computer?
- becoming defensive when confronted about gaming?
- losing track of time?
- preferring to spend more time with the computer than with friends or family?
- losing interest in previously important activities or hobbies?
- becoming socially isolated, moody, or irritable?
- establishing a new life with online friends?
- neglecting schoolwork and struggling to achieve acceptable grades?
- spending money on unexplained activities?
- attempting to hide gaming activities?[36-38]

Monitoring the amount of time and type of games played will help determine whether changes are needed. There are ways to set limits and encourage alternative behaviors in place of excessive video gaming. Consider these suggestions to redirect your child and help shift their behavior:

- **Go outside.** Encourage children to play outside, engage in physical activity, and interact with nature. Avoid using video game time as a reward. Children's brains are already programmed for the reward process with their computer time. Therefore, they need to be encouraged to develop other healthy activities, such as playing with pets in the yard, playing sports, going for a walk or run, or going to a park. In other words, leave the computer behind, and get outside for a breath of fresh air.

- **Keep track.** Eighty percent of the time a child spends on the computer has nothing to do with academics.[39] Put computers, smartphones, and other gaming devices in a central location, not behind closed doors, so that you can monitor activities. Learn how to check the computer's search history to confirm what your child has been doing on the internet.

- **Establish boundaries.** Set and enforce limits on screen time.[40] Children are often unable to accurately account for the time they have spent gaming, and the games induce children to continue playing. Try to limit gaming to less than an hour per day during the weekdays. If your child has become reliant on video games, begin by setting a goal of no more than one hour, gradually reducing the time each day until the goal is reached. In the meantime, learn how to set up firewalls, electronic limits, and blocks on cell phones and internet sites to further support your decisions.

- **Start talking.** Discuss internet use and gaming with your child, and encourage them to talk about their interests with you. Setting clear expectations will establish healthy communication and set an example for making good choices.[41]

- *Know your child.* If your child is doing well when participating in school, sports, and social activities, some gaming may be okay. Still, keep a close watch on the types of games they play and the frequency of use. If your child is experiencing challenges with anger or other disruptive behaviors, consider eliminating access to violent games.[42]

- *Get help.* For some children, gaming becomes an irresistible obsession. If your child shows signs of video game addiction, seek help and set limits. Depending on the level of the addiction, treatment options range from outpatient to inpatient programs.[43]

The Difference with Neurofeedback Games

Neurofeedback games function in a similar manner to all video gaming activities with some major exceptions. All video games use a reward system to keep the person engaged, and this capitalizes on children's willingness to participate in a neurofeedback training plan. The major exceptions for the programs we use in my clinics are (1) they are non-violent, (2) children participate for 30 minutes two or three times per week, (3) the 30-minute neurofeedback training plan includes multiple games of short duration, and (4) the neurofeedback video games have been scientifically developed to target auditory and visual processing weaknesses. All of these factors help ensure that we capitalize on the benefits of video gaming while minimizing the detrimental effects.

In the next few chapters, we'll put this understanding of how the brain can change to work as we look at the stories of children with processing problems. We'll see how identifying their specific challenges and developing a brain training intervention to address those challenges has allowed children to strengthen their processing abilities and transform their lives.

CHAPTER 6

AUDITORY PROCESSING PROBLEMS

As we delve into auditory processing problems, it's important to understand that they do not mean your child has intellectual limitations. These are two very different conditions, although they're often confused. Furthermore, auditory processing problems aren't about your child's hearing, which is a physical function. These difficulties are about your child's inability to process verbal information.[1,2]

As we explored in previous chapters, brain processing is similar to the way a computer processes input commands. Your child has to be able to accurately interpret auditory information to understand what has been said and know how to respond or what to do.

Children with auditory processing problems can have trouble with impulsivity, meaning they may find it difficult to stop, think, and avoid reacting automatically.[3] Your child may also have difficulty staying on-task, which can look like they're drifting off and not paying attention. Some children are unable to ignore distracting thoughts and feelings or distractions around them. Again, parents may interpret these types of behaviors as willful disobedience when this may not be true for these children.

To understand what this problem is like for your child, it can be helpful to think about the ways you interact with them. Most of your interactions are likely verbal. You talk to your child from the time they wake up until they go to sleep at night. You tell them what you want them to do. In the morning, you might tell them to get ready, brush their teeth, get their backpack, tie their shoes, remember their homework, feed the dog, and so on. On the drive to school, maybe you practice spelling words or discuss what needs to happen at school during the day, such as paying attention, listening to the teacher, doing what they're told to do, or staying out of trouble.

Think about all the verbal interactions your child encounters at home from start to finish. Now, think about all the things your child is told at school from peers and teachers in classrooms, the lunchroom, and on the playground. For parents who have working auditory processing skills, listening and paying attention to verbal information comes easily. For children without these processing skills, listening doesn't come so easily, and remembering what was said is often difficult or inconsistent. They can struggle to take notes in class. They have trouble remembering the list of things they were asked to do. Some children can't remember even one thing on the list. Having trouble following multi-step instructions is one of the telltale signs of weak auditory processing abilities.

In noisy settings, these children can appear lost. They can be distracted by sounds in a classroom such as another child swishing their feet, someone tapping a pencil, the lawnmower going by, the traffic outside, a noisy air conditioner, or other children talking around them. All sounds are treated equally in their brain, so any or all of these noises can interfere with their ability to focus. It's difficult for a child with auditory processing problems to discriminate between unimportant sounds and important sounds, such as what you or the teacher is saying.

Symptoms of auditory processing difficulties include the following:

- Difficulty paying attention in noisy environments
- Difficulty following long conversations

- Problems with reading comprehension
- Trouble understanding verbal math problems
- Difficulty remembering spoken information
- Difficulty taking notes
- Difficulty maintaining focus on an activity if other sounds are present
- Easily distracted by other sounds in the setting
- Difficulty following multi-step directions
- Difficulty directing, sustaining, or dividing attention
- Difficulty with reading, spelling, or both

Because these limitations can lead to extensive difficulties, it's important to figure out whether your child struggles with auditory processing. In my opinion, many mistakes are made when the differences between processing problems and intellectual abilities are confused. Children have been referred to special education for academic help when this type of support may not be what they need. This confusion has also led to medical diagnoses with related prescriptions that haven't resulted in meaningful long-term improvements.

Many children who struggle to learn in the general education classroom are referred to special education, but still don't do well. It's worth mentioning again that very intelligent and gifted children can fail in school or be referred to special education services because a distinction hasn't been made between processing problems and intellectual limitations or other types of learning disabilities.

As I mentioned before, processing problems can look like so many other conditions. Children have been diagnosed, or misdiagnosed, with ADD, ADHD, conduct disorder, behavioral disorders, oppositional defiant disorder (ODD), intermittent explosive disorder (IED), tics, intellectual/cognitive limitations, autism, Asperger's, executive functioning disorders, cognitive problems, Tourette's syndrome, and more.[4] Some children have multiple diagnoses, and some are pre-scribed psychotropic medications to manage their symptoms. It's important to note that the professionals providing these diagnoses are doing their best, but many of them simply don't understand the impact and symptoms of auditory processing. Without this, an effec-tive intervention is difficult to achieve.

The Significance of Auditory Processing Speed

Auditory processing speed can make a child appear to have a cognitive or developmental delay. A child with slower auditory processing *looks* like they're "slow." Prior to my work in this field, I also lacked an understanding of the significance of processing speed.

The term "slow" carries such negative connotations, making it a bit difficult to discuss, but it's important for parents to understand how processing speed can affect the way their child interacts with the world.

Slow auditory processing speed causes slow mental processing, which means a child's brain isn't keeping up with the speed of information they're receiving. They may have difficulty following a conversation and can seem lost when someone speaks quickly. So it can look like they're mentally slow or cognitively delayed.

In contrast, a child with fast auditory processing speed is seen as a quick study, able to respond quickly to a teacher's question, or keep up with a fast-paced conversation.

Abigail, the girl we first met in chapter 1, was one such child who struggled with auditory processing challenges. As you may recall, she was acting out in her kindergarten class and at home. She was distracted and disruptive, and her teacher said she was going to quit teaching because of this child. Nevertheless, Abigail was bright and determined. If her processing challenges could be identified and addressed, it might be possible to transform her learning and behavior struggles.

Abigail's Initial Assessment

Abigail and her grandmother came to my clinic for assessment and potential treatment. As with many of my clients, this began with an initial assessment that measures auditory and visual processing performance. We'll discuss this assessment in greater detail in a later chapter, but for now, I want to review the overall process of assessing and treating brain processing difficulties. In Abigail's case, this dealt with her auditory processing.

When I reviewed her initial assessment information, it became easier to understand why she was having such difficulties in school and at home. For her, many areas of auditory and visual processing were working well, with scores near the average range of 100. But the area of greatest concern was her auditory vigilance. In the first graph that follows, this score can be seen at the far left. Her scores in the areas of auditory vigilance, acuity, and elasticity were in the extremely impaired range. They showed that she had significant problems with remaining attentive when someone was talking to her, which affected her ability to process, remember, and follow through on what was said to her. These problems also caused her to tune out and drift off, to have problems getting back on track, and to become easily distracted.

As if that wasn't enough, her auditory comprehension and auditory persistence were impaired, causing additional difficulties with memory and slower reaction times (see second graph that follows). Abigail was between a rock and a hard place with regard to her ability to respond appropriately to verbal instructions or interact with the people around her. Her brain was simply overwhelmed when someone spoke to her.

In the graphs that follow, you can see the circled bars identifying the areas of brain processing that were not working well. (For descriptions of the IVA2 assessment areas, see Appendices B and C.)

Abigail's Initial Assessment Results

FS Attention Quotient = 67

Auditory	Visual
AQ = 56	AQ = 87

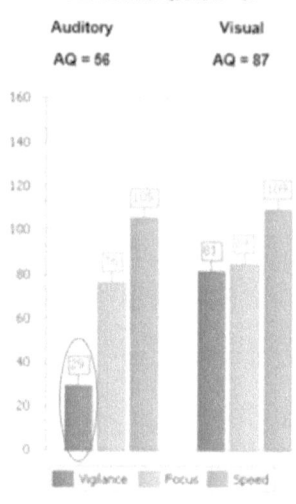

FS Response Control Quotient = 91

Auditory	Visual
RCQ = 89	RCQ = 95

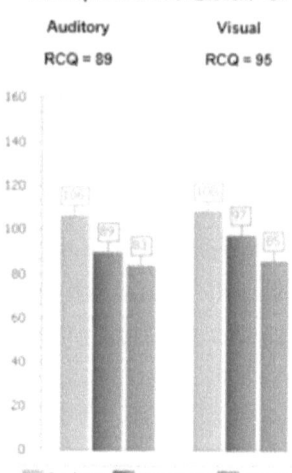

Sustained Auditory Attention Quotient = 39   Sustained Visual Attention Quotient = 101

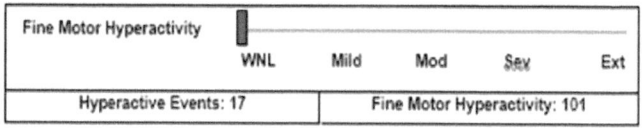

Fine Motor Hyperactivity					
	WNL	Mild	Mod	Sev	Ext

Hyperactive Events: 17	Fine Motor Hyperactivity: 101

Symptomatic	Raw	Quotient	WNL	Mild	Mod	Sev	Ext
Comprehension (A)	90.0%	72				▮	
Comprehension (V)	97.9%	109	▮				
Persistence (A)	50.8%	77			▮		
Persistence (V)	92.1%	95	▮				
Sensory/Motor (A)	210 ms	124	▮				
Sensory/Motor (V)	244 ms	111	▮				

What These Scores Meant for Abigail (and Those Around Her)

Remember that to manage our world, we need to be able to hang on to and remember both auditory and visual information. When we're unable to do so, we have far greater challenges than people who can process information well. For Abigail, this meant meltdowns of cataclysmic proportions. Her grandmother reported that family outings were ruined because Abigail was so disruptive. She couldn't be redirected and couldn't engage in behaviors appropriate for a seven-year-old. In short, she was a bright child, but no one wanted to be around her.

We developed a neurofeedback plan to target the areas of processing weakness identified in her initial assessment. The focus was primarily on her auditory processing difficulties. She participated in 40 sessions of neurofeedback intervention, and her reassessment results follow.

Abigail's Assessment After Neurofeedback

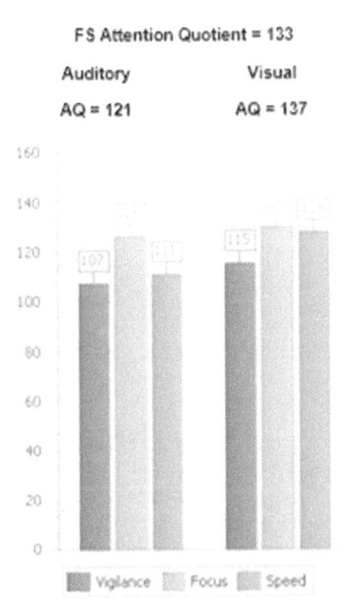

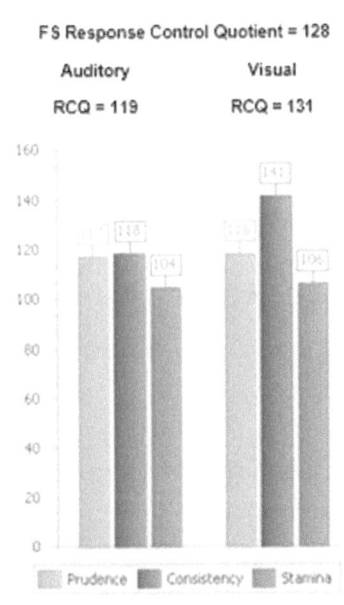

Fine Motor Hyperactivity					
WNL	Mild	Mod	Sev	Ext

Hyperactive Events: 6	Fine Motor Hyperactivity: 111

Symptomatic	Raw	Quotient	WNL	Mild	Mod	Sev	Ext
Comprehension (A)	100.0%	115					
Comprehension (V)	100.0%	116					
Persistence (A)	102.5%	105					
Persistence (V)	95.7%	96					
Sensory/Motor (A)	230 ms	120					
Sensory/Motor (V)	229 ms	116					

The changes in her assessment results were remarkable, as were the changes she experienced in her life. Her grandmother said they planned a family vacation, but while they were on the trip, she realized she had forgotten Abigail's ADHD medication. The grandmother nearly panicked, thinking the vacation would be ruined because of Abigail's tendency for disruptive behavior. But that wasn't the case. She remained well-behaved, she could be redirected when needed, and she didn't experience a single cataclysmic meltdown. The only question that remained in the grandmother's mind was whether Abigail still needed medication. That was a conversation they pursued with the family physician, who ultimately reduced the amount prescribed due to Abigail's improved attention, concentration, focus, and self-regulation.

Next is the story of a young boy who had been diagnosed with several conditions when his mother brought him to my clinic for an assessment.

Jeremy: Tantrums and Tics

Jeremy arrived at my clinic with his mother. He was in the fourth grade and had been identified as having autism and a speech and language impairment. Both Jeremy and his mother seemed very stressed, and their relationship seemed strong, but strained. His mother described her son as extremely bright, but unable to manage himself at school and in peer relationships. His negative behaviors included significant tantrums at school, disrespectful behavior toward his teacher, impulsively speaking out of turn in class, difficulty completing tasks and remaining focused, needing constant reminders, and facial tics. His mother said he made poor choices, and he was being disciplined for willful defiance in school. But he was also described as likable with a huge heart.

Jeremy's initial assessment results revealed significant deficits in his ability to process auditory information (see graphs on the next page). Although his visual processing scores were enough to be measurable, they also revealed some weaknesses. As a reference point, the vertical bars on the graph need to be near the 100-point mark for average processing abilities. Jeremy's auditory processing was extremely impaired, meaning he had very limited ability to remember any verbal information. This severe limitation was likely a contributing factor in his undesirable behaviors. He was a very intelligent boy who couldn't follow through and became agitated when people gave him verbal directions that he couldn't remember (i.e., process). (The term Invalid means he was unable to respond to the auditory and visual prompts during the assessment. The Invalid responses are interpreted as a zero per the assessment manual, which meant he didn't have enough auditory processing abilities to be measured.)

Jeremy's Initial Assessment Results

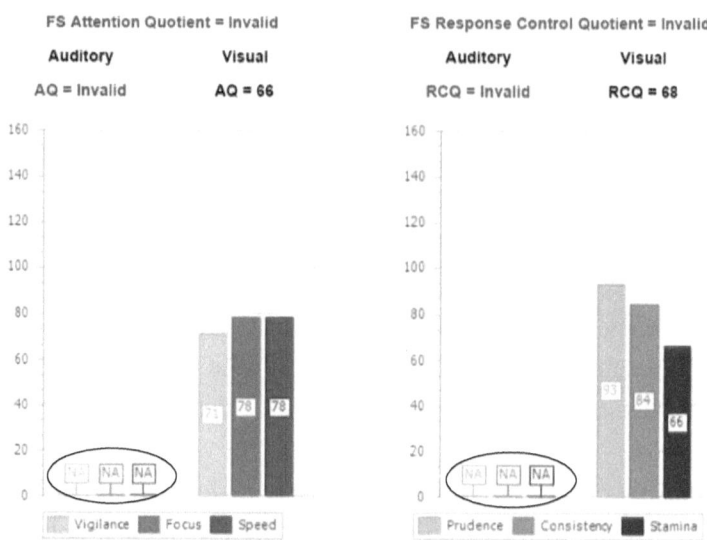

FS Attention Quotient = Invalid

Auditory	Visual
AQ = Invalid	AQ = 66

Vigilance · Focus · Speed

Sustained Auditory Attention Quotient = Invalid

FS Response Control Quotient = Invalid

Auditory	Visual
RCQ = Invalid	RCQ = 68

Prudence · Consistency · Stamina

Sustained Visual Attention Quotient = 56

Fine Motor Hyperactivity					
	WNL	Mild	Mod	Sev	Ext
Hyperactive Events: 119		Fine Motor Hyperactivity: 0			

Symptomatic	Raw	Quotient	WNL	Mild	Mod	Sev	Ext
Comprehension (A)	66.2%	0					
Comprehension (V)	87.9%	52					
Persistence (A)	120.5%	115					
Persistence (V)	88.6%	96					
Sensory/Motor (A)	331 ms	95					
Sensory/Motor (V)	240 ms	97					

When I explained these results to his mother, she had a better understanding of his inability to follow verbal instructions, as well as his acting out, temper tantrums, and impulsivity. Jeremy was also extremely impaired in fine motor hyperactivity, which caused him to get off task and be inattentive. His auditory and visual comprehension scores were in the extremely impaired range. Although he tested in the gifted range intellectually, he was unable to demonstrate his intellectual abilities, and his behavioral problems were directly related to his auditory and visual processing difficulties.

Jeremy's visual comprehension processing problems affected his ability to follow visual directions, properly compose letters, write legibly, and perform written math skills. His auditory comprehension processing problems affected his ability to understand verbal instructions and carry through on verbal assignments and tasks. This combination of challenges was a significant contributor to his extreme temper tantrums and problematic behaviors.

So we developed a neurofeedback plan to address these areas. With regular and consistent attendance, Jeremy completed 20 sessions (10 hours) of brain training and was reassessed.

The results of his second assessment (see graphs on the next page) reflected substantial changes in his ability to process auditory information. As a result, his behaviors began to improve at home and at school. However, his auditory vigilance score was still unmeasurable, and his auditory and visual comprehension scores remained extremely impaired, as did his fine motor hyperactivity score. So we developed a second neurofeedback intervention plan for him.

Jeremy's Second Assessment Results

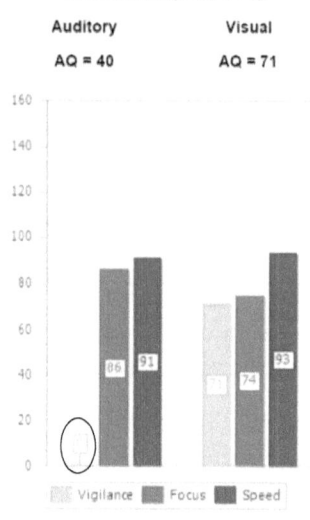

FS Attention Quotient = 52

Auditory	Visual
AQ = 40	AQ = 71

FS Response Control Quotient = 78

Auditory	Visual
RCQ = 75	RCQ = 88

Vigilance ■ Focus ■ Speed

Prudence ■ Consistency ■ Stamina

Sustained Auditory Attention Quotient = 0   **Sustained Visual Attention Quotient = 59**

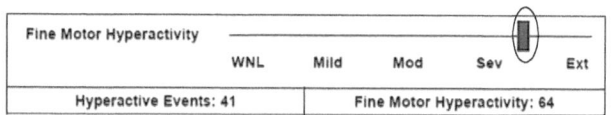

Fine Motor Hyperactivity					
	WNL	Mild	Mod	Sev	Ext
Hyperactive Events: 41			Fine Motor Hyperactivity: 64		

Symptomatic	Raw	Quotient	WNL	Mild	Mod	Sev	Ext
Comprehension (A)	74.6%	0					
Comprehension (V)	91.4%	70					
Persistence (A)	71.4%	86					
Persistence (V)	93.6%	98					
Sensory/Motor (A)	285 ms	103					
Sensory/Motor (V)	230 ms	102					

Following another 20 sessions of brain training, Jeremy's third assessment results reflected continued progress in his auditory processing abilities. His auditory vigilance score was near the average range. He also had significant improvement in his fine motor hyperactivity (see graph on the next page) with a score in the mildly impaired range. The remaining area of need was with his auditory comprehension, which was addressed with 20 more sessions of neurofeedback.

Jeremy's Third Assessment Results

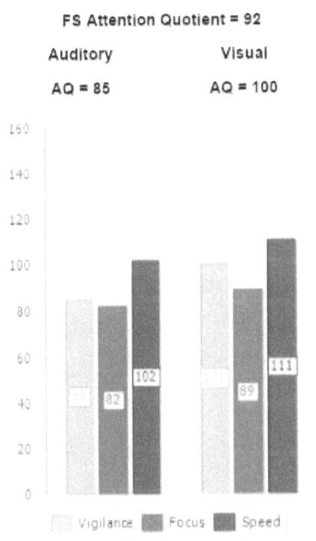

FS Attention Quotient = 92

Auditory	Visual
AQ = 85	AQ = 100

Sustained Auditory Attention Quotient = 64

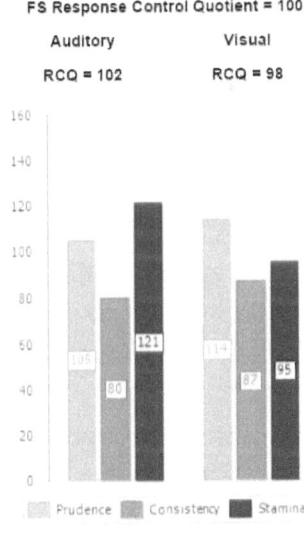

FS Response Control Quotient = 100

Auditory	Visual
RCQ = 102	RCQ = 98

Sustained Visual Attention Quotient = 101

Fine Motor Hyperactivity					
	WNL	Mild	Mod	Sev	Ext
Hyperactive Events: 22		Fine Motor Hyperactivity: 86			

Symptomatic	Raw	Quotient	WNL	Mild	Mod	Sev	Ext
Comprehension (A)	86.2%	0					
Comprehension (V)	97.9%	102					
Persistence (A)	82.2%	92					
Persistence (V)	125.7%	112					
Sensory/Motor (A)	238 ms	110					
Sensory/Motor (V)	183 ms	123					

Jeremy's mother expressed great appreciation for the changes in his behaviors at home and at school. Her son could pay attention much better, his temper tantrums were lessening in intensity and frequency, and his teachers saw improvements in his ability to complete his schoolwork.

Six months after completing his neurofeedback program, his mother requested a follow-up assessment (see graphs on next page). We found that Jeremy had continued to make gains. His initial areas of processing weaknesses had been resolved, and all assessed areas were functioning within the average or near average range. Ten areas were above average, and two areas were below average. His fine motor hyperactivity was within normal limits, and his auditory and visual comprehension scores were at the above-average level.

Jeremy's Six-Month Assessment

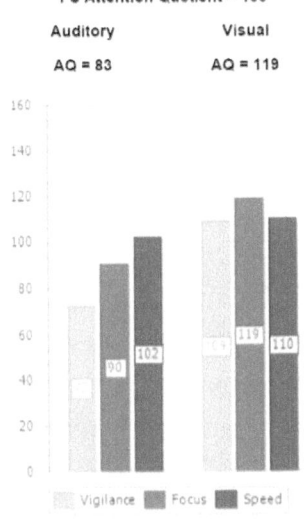

FS Attention Quotient = 100

Auditory	Visual
AQ = 83	AQ = 119

Sustained Auditory Attention Quotient = 92

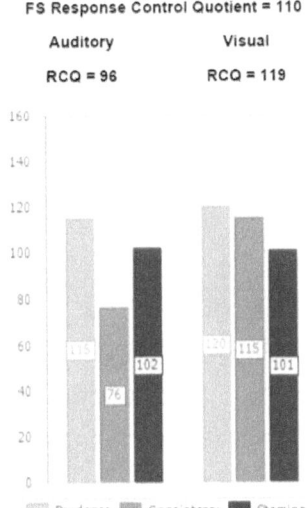

FS Response Control Quotient = 110

Auditory	Visual
RCQ = 96	RCQ = 119

Sustained Visual Attention Quotient = 117

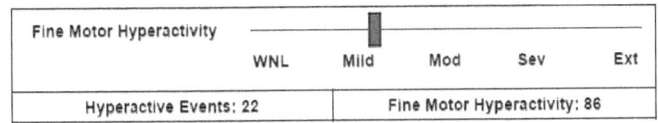

Fine Motor Hyperactivity				
WNL	Mild	Mod	Sev	Ext

Hyperactive Events: 22	Fine Motor Hyperactivity: 86

Symptomatic	Raw	Quotient	WNL	Mild	Mod	Sev	Ext
Comprehension (A)	86.2%	0					
Comprehension (V)	97.9%	102					
Persistence (A)	82.2%	92					
Persistence (V)	125.7%	112					
Sensory/Motor (A)	238 ms	110					
Sensory/Motor (V)	183 ms	123					

Jeremy's mother also reported a substantial difference in his ability to attend to others and his schoolwork, as well as a reduction in the physical tics that were assumed to be Tourette's syndrome, but never formally diagnosed. He was able to manage his emotions, and his tantrums were a thing of the past. Both Jeremy and his mother appeared more relaxed and genuinely seemed to enjoy each other's company. She said his progress and growth reflected how much he had changed since his first visit to the clinic.

Checklist for Auditory Processing Problems

If you're concerned that your child may have auditory processing problems, use the checklist that follows to identify their symptoms.

Which of the following auditory processing symptoms does your child have?

_____ Distracted in noisy places

_____ Difficulty staying on task

_____ Drifting off (mind seems to wander)

_____ Difficulty following long conversations

_____ Problems with reading comprehension

_____ Trouble understanding verbal math problems

_____ Difficulty remembering spoken information

_____ Difficulty taking notes

_____ Difficulty maintaining focus if other sounds are present

_____ Easily distracted

_____ Difficulty with organizational skills

_____ Difficulty following directions

_____ Struggles to remember multi-step verbal instructions

_____ Difficulty paying attention

_____ Difficulty with reading, spelling, or both

_____ Difficulty remaining alert

_____ Difficulty getting back on task

_____ Tendency to "tune out" when listening to others speak

_____ Difficulty directing, sustaining, or dividing attention

If your child has four or more of these symptoms, they may be struggling with auditory processing problems.

CHAPTER 7

VISUAL PROCESSING PROBLEMS

Visual processing problems can significantly interfere with your child's ability to learn. They cause struggles with tasks like organizing, picking up toys and putting them away, learning spelling words by sight, performing math calculations, and reading comprehension. They also frequently cause children to miss letters when writing words, struggle to copy words and information from a whiteboard or other source,[1] struggle to remember letters and numbers as if they have short- or long-term memory problems,[2] and struggle to recall information presented visually. As with auditory processing problems, visual processing problems are often diagnosed as ADHD.

These problems aren't about your child's vision, however, which is a physical function.[3] Remember that they're an inability to process visual information.[4,5] Your child has to be able to accurately interpret the information to understand what has been shown to them and know how to respond.

Children with visual processing problems have difficulty remaining attentive to visual tasks,[6] struggle with visual memory and spatial orientation,[7] and can be easily distracted by too much visual stimulation.[8] They can appear disorganized, frequently lose or misplace things, trip or bump into things, reverse letters when writing, or mix up numbers when trying to do math problems. Some children have difficulty writing spelling words or seem to have trouble following directions that were shown to them. Others have eye/hand coordination challenges. Still other children may have trouble remembering what they read or may seem unable to remember what they learned the day before or even a few minutes ago.

Visual processing difficulties can include a range of symptoms:

- Difficulty with tasks that require copying (taking notes)
- Written copies may be missing words
- Often cannot remember even basic facts about material read silently
- Below-average reading or writing
- Below-average math skills; may ignore function signs, omitting steps
- May confuse visually similar information
- May fail to notice changes in bulletin board displays, signs, or posted notices[9]

The images that follow are writing examples of children with visual processing problems.

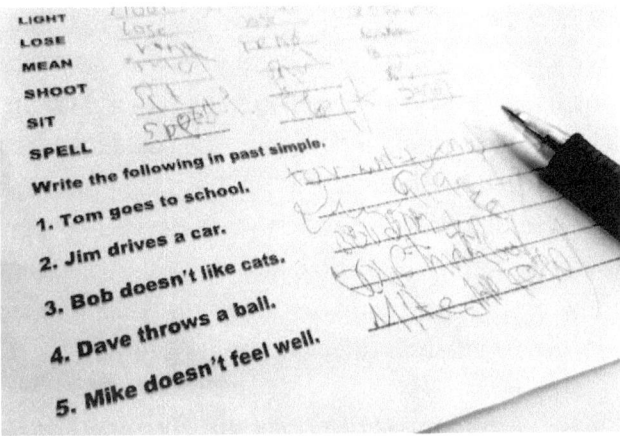

To better understand what this problem is like for your child, think about the ways we depend on visual processing throughout the day. Most of us take these abilities for granted, not realizing how much we rely on them. Your child needs visual processing abilities to remember visual information and for good visual memory, which helps them do math calculations, write spelling words, remember how to get home, use a calculator, put away toys, make a bed, put dishes in the dishwasher, wash dishes, take out the trash, use the microwave, remember where they left their shoes, or remember where they put their homework, among endless other tasks.

Obviously, weak visual processing can affect your child in many areas of learning and life. As a result, these problems can cause anxiety and poor behaviors. So children might act out, be disruptive, be argumentative, have temper tantrums, fail to pay attention, become easily frustrated, and struggle to focus on tasks or follow along.

Let's discuss Zoe, who had difficulty learning and was failing in school.

Zoe: When Initial Interventions Don't Work

Zoe and her siblings were being raised by their grandmother. We had worked with two of her siblings when the grandmother requested services for Zoe, a very sweet seven-year-old. She had difficulty learning to read and couldn't understand her schoolwork regardless of how hard she tried. When I assesssed her, the reason became clear. She was unable to process visual information. She could follow along when given verbal instructions, but she was unable to complete school tasks, causing her to fall behind more and more as the years progressed. Her grandmother was deeply concerned, and rightfully so.

The following are her initial assessment results that reflect extreme impairments across all areas of visual processing.

Zoe's Initial Assessment Results

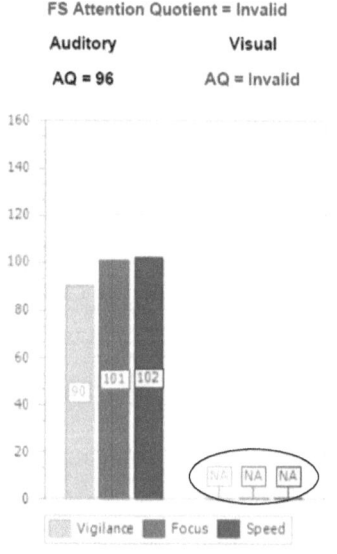

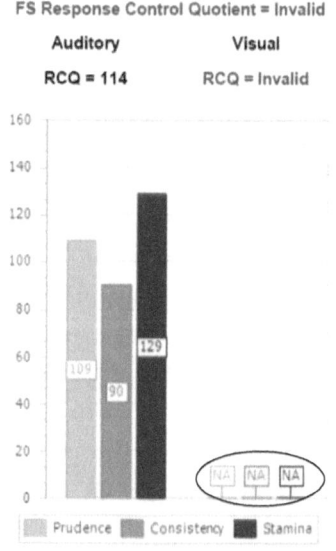

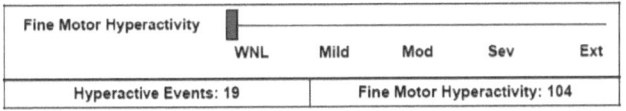

			WNL	Mild	Mod	Sev	Ext
Fine Motor Hyperactivity							

Hyperactive Events: 19	Fine Motor Hyperactivity: 104

Symptomatic	Raw	Quotient	WNL	Mild	Mod	Sev	Ext
Comprehension (A)	96.2%	102					
Comprehension (V)	67.1%	25					
Persistence (A)	64.8%	87					
Persistence (V)	88.5%	93					
Sensory/Motor (A)	345 ms	105					
Sensory/Motor (V)	359 ms	93					

Although Zoe had strong auditory processing abilities with scores falling in the average to superior range, her visual processing scores were so low that they couldn't be measured. (The term Invalid means she was unable to respond to the visual prompts during the assessment. The Invalid responses are interpreted as a zero per the assessment manual, which meant she didn't have enough processing abilities to be measured.)

When children are unable to process visual information, they can look disorganized, have difficulty learning how to read and do math, and are often unable to follow visual instructions. In Zoe's case, her visual processing abilities weren't strong enough for her to learn how to read. Her visual comprehension score in the extremely impaired range meant it was nearly impossible for her to understand any information that was presented visually.

Based on her assessment results, we developed a neurofeedback plan and reassessed her after 20 sessions (10 hours) of consistent brain training. The assessment results (see graphs on the next page) revealed only minimal improvement in the areas of concern.

Zoe's Second Assessment Results

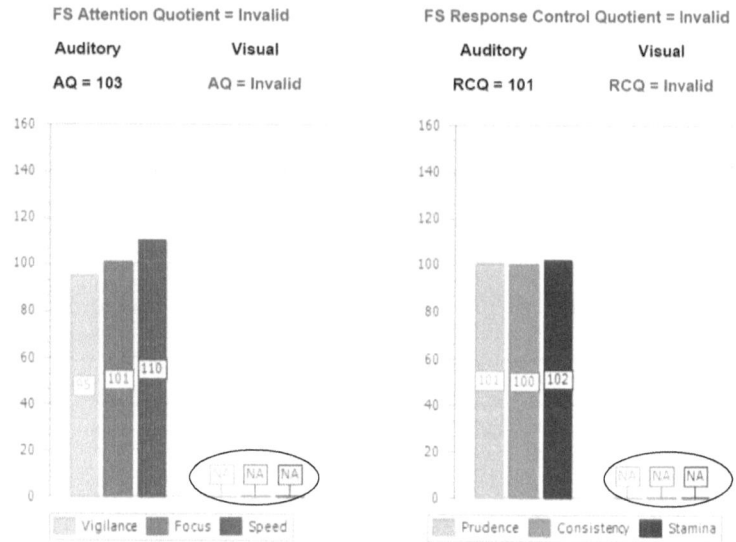

Sustained Auditory Attention Quotient = 98   Sustained Visual Attention Quotient = Invalid

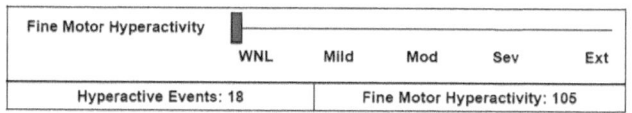

Fine Motor Hyperactivity	WNL	Mild	Mod	Sev	Ext
Hyperactive Events: 18	Fine Motor Hyperactivity: 105				

Symptomatic	Raw	Quotient	WNL	Mild	Mod	Sev	Ext
Comprehension (A)	97.7%	107					
Comprehension (V)	73.6%	43					
Persistence (A)	115.8%	109					
Persistence (V)	114.0%	102					
Sensory/Motor (A)	360 ms	103					
Sensory/Motor (V)	333 ms	98					

To her credit, Zoe's grandmother was persistent about continuing treatment. After Zoe completed another 20 sessions, her reassessment continued to show limited results.

Her results (or seeming lack thereof) were different from our prior experiences with children. Generally, by the time they have completed 40 sessions, children respond to the intervention. But Zoe persisted with the intervention even though it appeared that her functioning had worsened (see graphs of her third assessment). Still, her grandmother reported seeing changes and wanted to continue, stating she wouldn't give up on her youngest granddaughter. So the next intervention plan continued to focus on her areas of weakness.

Zoe's Third Assessment Results

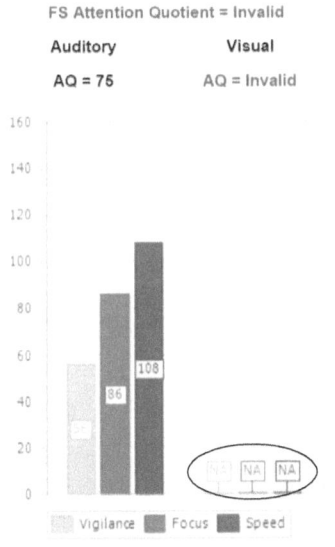

Sustained Auditory Attention Quotient = 53

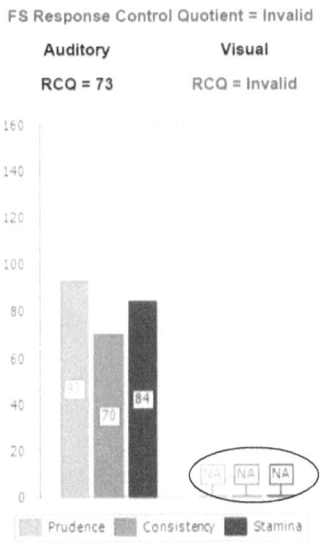

Sustained Visual Attention Quotient = Invalid

Fine Motor Hyperactivity					
	WNL	Mild	Mod	Sev	Ext

Hyperactive Events: 72	Fine Motor Hyperactivity: 52

Symptomatic	Raw	Quotient	WNL	Mild	Mod	Sev	Ext
Comprehension (A)	76.9%	36					
Comprehension (V)	58.6%	0					
Persistence (A)	121.2%	111					
Persistence (V)	106.5%	99					
Sensory/Motor (A)	345 ms	105					
Sensory/Motor (V)	322 ms	100					

Finally, Zoe's brain began to respond to the neurofeedback interventions in a remarkable way (see graphs on the next page). Her visual processing started to function for the first time in her life. The clinicians and her grandmother expressed cheers and tears of joy. Zoe was all smiles as she was blossoming into an amazing little girl who could now follow along in school. She developed self-confidence, stood and walked taller, and smiled more often. She was transforming before our very eyes. Her grandmother expressed deep appreciation for the support and encouragement she was given during the process of working with Zoe. Although it took longer than expected, she persevered and gained a better quality of life and a brighter future for herself.

Zoe's Fourth Assessment Results

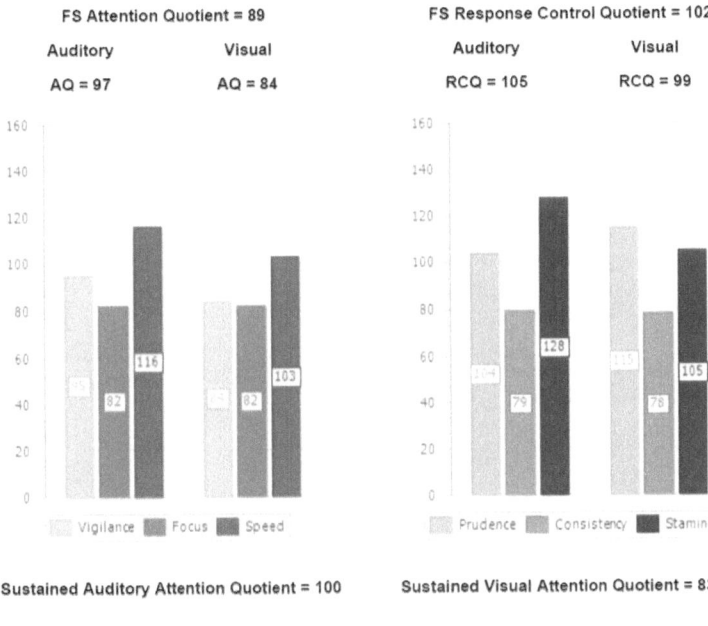

FS Attention Quotient = 89		FS Response Control Quotient = 102	
Auditory	Visual	Auditory	Visual
AQ = 97	AQ = 84	RCQ = 105	RCQ = 99

Vigilance Focus Speed

Prudence Consistency Stamina

Sustained Auditory Attention Quotient = 100   Sustained Visual Attention Quotient = 83

Fine Motor Hyperactivity	WNL	Mild	Mod	Sev	Ext

Hyperactive Events: 11	Fine Motor Hyperactivity: 112

Symptomatic	Raw	Quotient	WNL	Mild	Mod	Sev	Ext
Comprehension (A)	99.2%	112					
Comprehension (V)	92.9%	99					
Persistence (A)	107.0%	105					
Persistence (V)	108.5%	100					
Sensory/Motor (A)	371 ms	102					
Sensory/Motor (V)	369 ms	90					

We conducted a four-month follow-up assessment (see the next graph), which continued to show ongoing improvements similar to other clients who have said their lives continued to improve months after completion of the neurofeedback training program.

Zoe's Assessment Results Fourth Months after Treatment

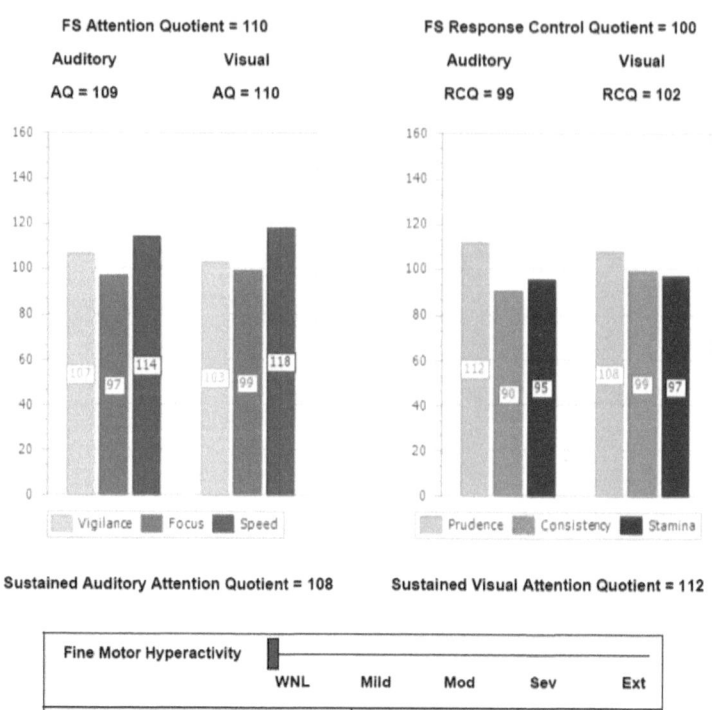

FS Attention Quotient = 110

Auditory	Visual
AQ = 109	AQ = 110

FS Response Control Quotient = 100

Auditory	Visual
RCQ = 99	RCQ = 102

Sustained Auditory Attention Quotient = 108   Sustained Visual Attention Quotient = 112

Fine Motor Hyperactivity					
	WNL	Mild	Mod	Sev	Ext
Hyperactive Events: 4	Fine Motor Hyperactivity: 119				

Symptomatic	Raw	Quotient	WNL	Mild	Mod	Sev	Ext
Comprehension (A)	97.7%	107	▌				
Comprehension (V)	99.3%	118	▌				
Persistence (A)	60.6%	86			▌		
Persistence (V)	98.3%	97	▌				
Sensory/Motor (A)	329 ms	107	▌				
Sensory/Motor (V)	322 ms	100	▌				

Zoe again returned 21 months after treatment for a follow-up assessment (see the next graphs), and we were pleased to see her results continued to remain stable with only minor areas of fluctuation. Her grandmother reported that she was excelling in school.

Zoe's Assessment Results 21 Months after Treatment

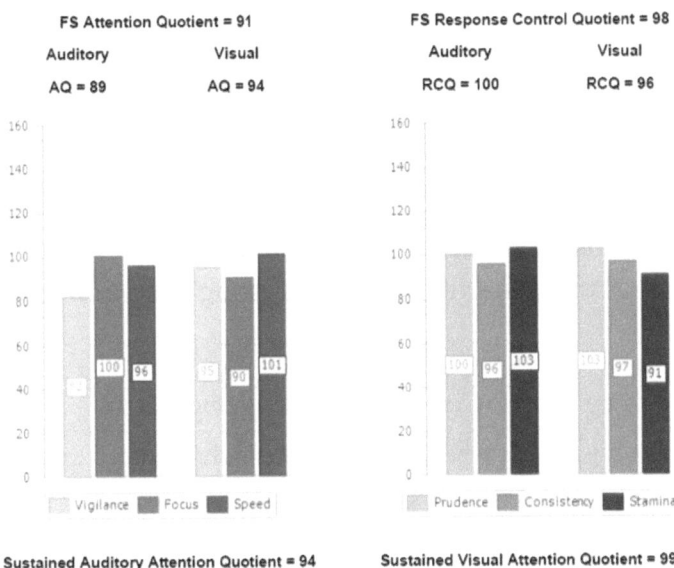

FS Attention Quotient = 91

Auditory   Visual

AQ = 89   AQ = 94

FS Response Control Quotient = 98

Auditory   Visual

RCQ = 100   RCQ = 96

Sustained Auditory Attention Quotient = 94   Sustained Visual Attention Quotient = 99

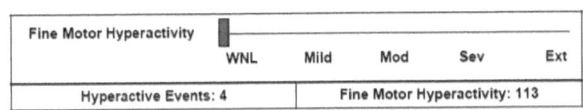

Fine Motor Hyperactivity					
	WNL	Mild	Mod	Sev	Ext
Hyperactive Events: 4	Fine Motor Hyperactivity: 113				

Symptomatic	Raw	Quotient	WNL	Mild	Mod	Sev	Ext
Comprehension (A)	99.2%	108					
Comprehension (V)	97.9%	102					
Persistence (A)	74.9%	88					
Persistence (V)	85.1%	94					
Sensory/Motor (A)	359 ms	93					
Sensory/Motor (V)	265 ms	99					

As you can see, Zoe continued to improve across the range of markers for auditory and visual processing. By the time this final assessment was completed, she was progressing in school, her self-esteem and self-confidence were also much improved, and her reading abilities and grades were better. The credit for her improvement goes to everyone involved in supporting her, to her grandmother who continued to believe in Zoe, and particularly to Zoe for her desire to succeed even though it took longer than she hoped it would.

Checklist for Visual Processing Problems

If you're concerned your child may have visual processing problems, use this checklist to identify their symptoms.

Which of the following visual processing symptoms does your child have?

_____ Missing letters when writing or copying words

_____ Missing words when writing or copying sentences or phrases

_____ Disorganized

_____ Difficulty remembering basic facts about material read silently

_____ Easily distracted by visual activities in the room

_____ Below average reading or writing but strong verbal skills

_____ Frequently loses or misplaces things

_____ Math skills below average

_____ Ignoring math function signs

_____ Omitting steps or confuses visually similar information

_____ Mixing up numbers when trying to do math

_____ Failing to notice changes in bulletin board displays, signs, or posted notices

_____ Tripping or bumping into things frequently

_____ Difficulty organizing the bedroom or make the bed

_____ Trouble with eye/hand coordination

_____ Struggling to pick up toys and put them away

_____ Inability to write legibly

_____ Trouble writing spelling words correctly, but can spell the words correctly out loud

If your child has four or more of these symptoms, they may be struggling with visual processing problems.

CHAPTER 8

COMBINED AUDITORY AND VISUAL PROCESSING PROBLEMS

As we have seen, children with auditory processing problems struggle to remember verbal information, affecting their ability to remember and follow through. They have trouble with impulsivity, difficulty staying on-task, are unable to ignore distracting thoughts and feelings or distracting things going on around them, have difficulty paying attention in noisy environments, have trouble following long conversations, struggle with reading comprehension, and have difficulty understanding verbal math problems.

Children with visual processing problems can be disorganized, have trouble learning spelling words by sight, struggle to perform math calculations, have difficulty with reading comprehension, miss letters when writing words, and have trouble copying words and information from a whiteboard.[1] They may struggle to remember letters and numbers as if they have short- or long-term memory problems[2] and may have difficulty recalling information presented visually.

Children with both auditory and visual processing problems struggle even more. They encounter numerous challenges in their social and learning environments. Because they can't rely on stronger abilities in either form of processing, they don't have a "fallback" position to learn.

For example, if a child can process auditory information, but has visual processing problems, parents and teachers can adjust how they provide information by switching to visual instructions. Visual cues such as making lists and demonstrating information can help a child with auditory problems. Likewise, for children with visual processing problems, parents and teachers can switch to verbal instructions and play to the child's greater verbal processing strengths. For the child who is unable to process both verbal and visual information, learning is especially difficult.

These are the children who are unable to follow through on most instructions. They may look lost with a vacant look in their eyes, and they can appear to be cognitively or developmentally delayed. Most people who encounter a child with both auditory and visual processing problems have a sense that something is "off." They seem to have trouble grasping what's happening around them and are most likely to be referred to special education because the general education classroom is too overwhelming for them. Importantly, though, once the auditory and visual processing problems are identified and treated, these children can typically return to the general education classroom and thrive in their academic and personal lives, as you will see in the following story about Jasmine.

Jasmine: Disconnected and Disengaged

Fifteen-year-old Jasmine was described by everyone who knew her as a sweet girl with a pretty smile, but when I looked into her eyes, it was as if she wasn't there. She seemed vacant and empty, and she had a look of "grayness" about her. She was there, but at the same time, she wasn't. She responded politely, though minimally, when she was spoken to, but she wouldn't start a conversation.

Her family was concerned about her future and openly wondered how she would do after high school. They described her as always having been this way. While she was pleasant and cooperative, they felt she wasn't living the robust and engaged life they wanted for her. She seemed to go through the motions of her daily life, but was somehow disconnected and disengaged.

Jasmine's initial assessment revealed significant limitations in her ability to process auditory and visual information. This meant she was unable to respond effectively to either auditory or visual prompts during the assessment. These findings were coupled with extremely impaired levels of hyperactivity, as well as extremely impaired auditory and visual comprehension. A child with this particular combination of limitations is unable to effectively connect with their world and can appear to be cognitively delayed, which were the descriptors Jasmine's family identified during the intake.

In her first assessment, she had multiple invalid scores. (The term Invalid means she was unable to respond to the auditory and visual prompts during the assessment. The Invalid responses are interpreted as a zero per the assessment manual, which meant she didn't have enough processing abilities to be measured.)

Jasmine's Initial Assessment

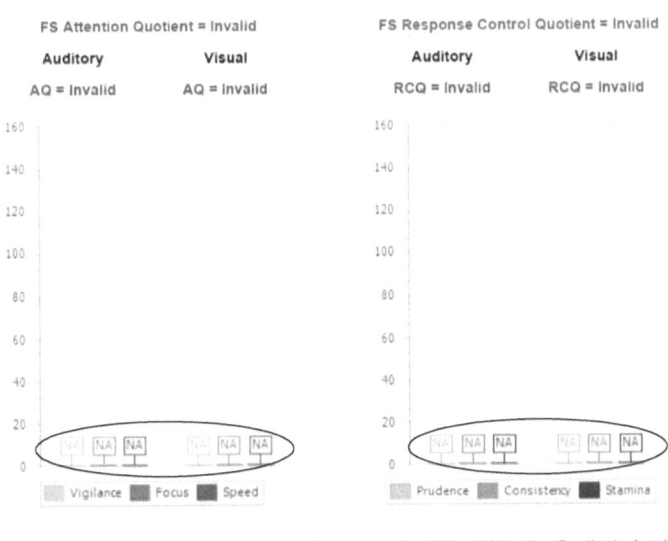

FS Attention Quotient = Invalid

Auditory   Visual

AQ = Invalid   AQ = Invalid

Vigilance   Focus   Speed

FS Response Control Quotient = Invalid

Auditory   Visual

RCQ = Invalid   RCQ = Invalid

Prudence   Consistency   Stamina

Sustained Auditory Attention Quotient = Invalid   Sustained Visual Attention Quotient = Invalid

Fine Motor Hyperactivity						
	WNL	Mild	Mod	Sev	Ext	
Hyperactive Events: 13			Fine Motor Hyperactivity: 28			

Symptomatic	Raw	Quotient	WNL	Mild	Mod	Sev	Ext
Comprehension (A)	67.7%	0					
Comprehension (V)	63.6%	0					
Persistence (A)	102.0%	105					
Persistence (V)	98.0%	107					
Sensory/Motor (A)	251 ms	108					
Sensory/Motor (V)	229 ms	94					

Jasmine was extremely impaired in fine motor hyperactivity, leading her to get off-task and have difficulty remaining attentive. (This type of hyperactivity isn't to be confused with the hyperactivity of children who can't remain still in their seats, are in constant motion, or are physically impulsive, which she was not.) A child with scores in the average or above average range would be described as being able to maintain attention.

As indicated in the graph above, Jasmine was very impaired in auditory and visual comprehension, which meant she had difficulty tracking and understanding what was being said and shown to her. As previously mentioned, this type of processing problem isn't about intellectual limitations, although children with these issues are often categorized as such. The remainder of Jasmine's scores were in the average range.

Based on the initial assessment data, we developed and implemented a neurofeedback intervention plan. Jasmine attended twice per week for 20 sessions and was reassessed using the same assessments (see graphs on next page). Her reassessed results were remarkable, revealing significant improvement across all areas where she was previously unable to respond to both auditory and visual processing prompts. She improved from extremely impaired across all markers to functioning in the average or near-average range both auditorily and visually. Most importantly, both her auditory and visual comprehension scores had improved from the extremely impaired range to within normal limits. Her fine motor hyperactivity score remained in the extremely impaired range, and her scores on auditory persistence and auditory sensory/motor were in the mildly impaired range.

Jasmine's Second Assessment

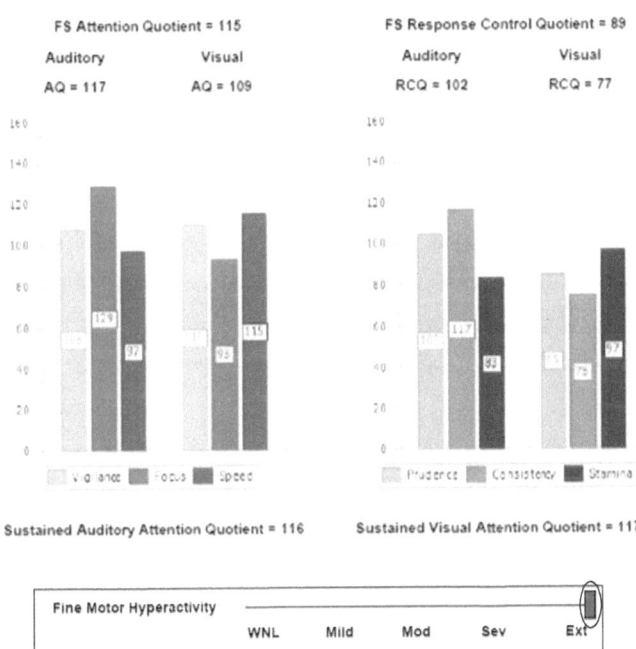

Symptomatic	Raw	Quotient	WNL	Mild	Mod	Sev	Ext
Comprehension (A)	100.0%	106	▮				
Comprehension (V)	100.0%	105	▮				
Persistence (A)	73.8%	85		⬭			
Persistence (V)	97.7%	106	▮				
Sensory/Motor (A)	369 ms	84		⬭			
Sensory/Motor (V)	213 ms	103	▮				

Given the significant changes, you might wonder whether the initial assessment was accurate. To verify the validity of each assessment, we obtained additional information about how she was functioning in her life. In Jasmine's situation, it's worth noting how much she had changed in physical appearance after her initial intake. She demonstrated greater self-confidence, made better eye contact, and responded with more alertness in conversations. The look in her eyes was that of a bright and engaged young woman. Her family members remarked that she was "like a different person." She seemed happy and engaged with her life. She was performing better in school and developing more in-depth relationships with peers and family members. The family expressed deep gratitude for the neurofeedback treatment.

Even though Jasmine made tremendous progress in the first 20 sessions, there was more room for improvement of her fine motor hyperactivity, which was still in the extremely impaired range. The family decided to continue with another 20 sessions to focus more directly on her brain's hyperactivity. So, we implemented a second treatment plan.

Her third assessment results document that her hyperactivity improved from extremely impaired to within normal limits, and her auditory persistence was within the average range, although her auditory sensory/motor score was in the mild to moderately impaired range (see graphs on following page).

Jasmine's Third Assessment

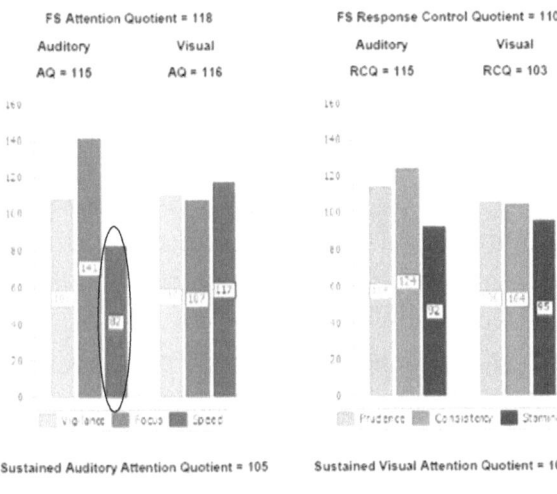

<table>
<tr><td>FS Attention Quotient = 118</td><td>FS Response Control Quotient = 110</td></tr>
</table>

Auditory	Visual	Auditory	Visual
AQ = 115	AQ = 116	RCQ = 115	RCQ = 103

Vigilance · Focus · Speed   Prudence · Consistency · Stamina

Sustained Auditory Attention Quotient = 105   Sustained Visual Attention Quotient = 105

Fine Motor Hyperactivity					
	WNL	Mild	Mod	Sev	Ext

Hyperactive Events: 1	Fine Motor Hyperactivity: 107

Symptomatic	Raw	Quotient	WNL	Mild	Mod	Sev	Ext
Comprehension (A)	99.2%	94					
Comprehension (V)	99.3%	94					
Persistence (A)	98.7%	103					
Persistence (V)	85.0%	91					
Sensory/Motor (A)	395 ms	79					
Sensory/Motor (V)	208 ms	106					

At the beginning of treatment, Jasmine had been conditionally diagnosed with ADHD. Following completion of 40 sessions (20 hours), no significant impairment was found in her ability to sustain attention in all assessed areas. In other words, her ADHD symptoms had resolved. Although she had two remaining areas of mild to moderate impairment on her auditory speed and auditory sensory motor scores, Jasmine and her parents were delighted with her accomplishments and how well she was able to function in her life.

The changes that took place were very encouraging. Identifying her auditory and visual processing problems and using neurofeedback to strengthen these areas of her brain processing resulted in a different life course for Jasmine.

Children with combined processing challenges can demonstrate a range of symptoms. If you're concerned that your child falls into this category, you may wish to consider the checklists at the end of each of the previous two chapters.

Chapters 6, 7, and 8 have considered the assessment and intervention process for children with combined and specific auditory or visual processing problems. As the stories demonstrate, this process can have transformative effects for children who struggle with learning, attention, and behavior. The next chapters delve into the neurofeedback process itself, describing how it works and how the Integrated Visual and Auditory-2 (IVA2) assessment helps us identify and treat processing challenges.

Remote Neurofeedback Services

Remote neurofeedback services provide access to the same services available in my clinics but you participate from home. You work with a clinician at a scheduled time and receive the same assessments and neurofeedback services as if you were attending in person.

A free 15-minute consultation can be scheduled to discuss the technology and licensing requirements for remote services. Some limitations may exist depending on internet speed and other factors.

Contact Dr. Connie McReynolds for more information.

Email: connie@mcreyno.com

Website: www.conniemcreynolds.com

Educational Consultation Services

Educational consultation services are available to obtain guidance on 504, IEP, and ISP service plans to support your child at school.

Even if your child does not qualify for a 504, IEP or ISP plan, it may be beneficial to identify the types of accommodations and learning supports that will enhance your child's ability to succeed in school.

Without a true understanding of the way auditory and visual processing problems affect your child's ability to learn, parents (and teachers) are often at a loss as to how to help children succeed at home and in school.

Contact Dr. Connie McReynolds to schedule a free 15-minute discovery call.

Email: connie@mcreyno.com

Website: www.conniemcreynolds.com

CHAPTER 9

NEUROFEEDBACK AND THE IVA2 ASSESSMENT

Based on more than a decade of work, children I have worked with in my neurofeedback clinics have reported that they are *"able to pay attention even when they don't want to . . ."* and *"choose whether to focus on what their friends are saying in the classroom or listen to the teacher."* They have gone from earning poor grades to passing grades, some excelling to the honor roll for the first time in their academic lives. Through our effective assessment process and use of artifact corrected neurofeedback interventions, the resulting improvements in attentional auditory and visual processing abilities have led to better results in academic work, decreased behavioral interventions, and improved family dynamics.[1] (See Appendix A for more information about artifact corrected neurofeedback.)

Again, neurofeedback works by retraining the brain, similar to the way the body is strengthened by exercise. To make lasting changes to the brain or to develop a positive habit in place of a negative one, it takes repeating the new pattern consistently and long enough to develop new wiring in the brain.

Everything you've ever learned from walking, talking, chewing gum, riding a bike, eating, and drinking happened through repetition. As a child when you were learning how to write, you practiced how to hold the pencil, how to form letters and numbers correctly, and how to write sentences and paragraphs. Learning spelling words, doing math, reading, singing, and climbing were all accomplished through practice and repetition. And you needed feedback on how you were doing. The learning process can be slow, but once your brain is trained, it tends to keep the patterning.

Neurofeedback retrains brain wave patterns using the principles of operant conditioning, which means learning occurs by using reinforcement and repetition to produce desired changes. It provides a type of shortcut to boosting brain functions by teaching your child how to better regulate their brain, which helps to empower them and build self-awareness. Because the brain can be trained to produce a desired effect, it's possible to reduce hyperactivity, improve concentration, and enhance attention and memory.[2,3] As I've said, neurofeedback has been scientifically proven as an effective treatment for symptoms of ADHD[4] or other learning difficulties,[5-12] and the effects can be lasting.[13-15]

Neurofeedback combines EEG (electroencephalogram) technology and computers to capture and display nearly instantaneous information (feedback) about a person's brain waves. Since it doesn't involve adding any substances to the body, it's considered a safe and effective, non-invasive, alternative treatment for ADHD.

Brain wave activity is detected using EEG sensors, but the sensors don't send signals back to the brain, which is why neurofeedback is considered non-invasive. Brain wave signals are sent to the computer, which then interact with computer programs known as neurofeedback video games. The sensors monitor the brain waves while your child interacts with the specially designed games.

The amount of training needed differs from child to child, and results vary. Ultimately, everyone requires an individualized approach, which we design using data from the initial intake and the Integrated Visual and Auditory-2 (IVA2) assessment.

How Neurofeedback Sessions Work

Neurofeedback training is typically done in 30-minute sessions, two or three times per week for 20 sessions. Then, a reassessment is done to determine the progress on goals. As you've seen in the case studies you've already read, the number of total sessions can vary depending on the conditions being treated and how the child's brain responds to the process.

Sensors are placed on the child's scalp in specific locations depending on therapy goals. The process is painless.

Neurofeedback works by gradually training the brain to change in targeted ways by reinforcing positive pathways (roadmaps). Children play the specifically designed video games, which help them train their brain in a fun way.

Once the brain learns a new skill or new way of functioning, it tends to maintain those changes. Again, this is similar to learning how to ride a bike. Even if you haven't ridden in years, your brain will still remember how to do it.

Your child may initially experience mild side effects of fatigue or irritability after neurofeedback, which is the result of beginning a brain training process. This is similar to the muscle soreness and fatigue you might experience after starting a new exercise program. The brain gets tired, too. These mild side effects generally go away after a few sessions.

Through the use of a systematic approach to brain training, children can boost their brain performance to improve their auditory and visual processing, which leads to better grades, fewer behavioral interventions, and improved social-emotional functioning.

The IVA2 Assessment

To build an effective and individual neurofeedback plan, we must first assess a person's baseline processing abilities. The Integrated Visual and Auditory Continuous Performance Test (IVA2 CPT) is an assessment of visual and auditory attention and impulse control in children and adults.[16] It identifies the causal factors interfering with a child's ability to learn, remember, and adapt in school and at home. In my opinion, any elementary school age child showing signs of learning or attention problems would benefit from the information gained by taking this assessment.

The IVA2 assessment is computer-based and takes about 20 minutes to complete. It presents the child with auditory and visual prompts that require them to respond to instructions by clicking the mouse. The prompts randomly alternate between auditory and visual. The randomness means it's almost impossible to predict what will come next. In this way, the assessment provides reliable information on their ability to sustain attention.

The assessment measures impulsivity and inattention in five ways to identify strengths and weaknesses affecting the child's ability to process auditory and visual information:

- *Focused Attention*—The ability to make correct responses to specific auditory and visual target stimuli, which is reported primarily by the Vigilance and Prudence scales.

- *Sustained Attention*—The maintenance of a stable and reliable response pattern is measured by the variability of reaction time reported in the areas of Stamina, Consistency, and Focus, and reported in the global scales of Auditory and Visual Sustained Attention.

- *Selective Attention*—The ability to accurately demonstrate the mental set of internalized rules necessary for inhibiting and responding to stimuli. The Prudence, Vigilance, and Comprehension Scales are reflective of this element.

- *Alternating Attention*—The use of mental flexibility skills required to shift sets between competing demands for attention.

Differences in the visual and auditory scores for the Speed, Consistency, and Focus scales may reflect strengths or weaknesses in this aspect.

- *Divided Attention*—The ability to accurately process and respond to two or more different tasks simultaneously. The instructions specify needing to balance both accuracy and speed of responding. Differences in the Prudence and Speed scales may indicate problems or strengths in this domain.[17]

The IVA2 assessment is used to determine the child's baseline levels of auditory and visual functioning. The results generate a 15-page report that identifies the child's strengths and weaknesses. Some children are unable to respond to either visual or auditory prompts due to extreme deficits in attentional functioning. When this happens, the word Invalid appears on the assessment report and is interpreted as a "zero" per the assessment rules.[18]

Through the identification of auditory and visual processing problems unique to each child, we create an intervention plan to strengthen the identified areas of weaknesses. For example, a child who has difficulty remembering what was said will have a plan that focuses on enhancing auditory memory.

Reassessment occurs after every 20 sessions of brain training to measure the child's progress in strengthening auditory and visual processing abilities. (See Appendices A and B for descriptions of the assessment scales.)

The information from the IVA2 assessment can also lead to specific classroom interventions targeted to support learning (see chapter 12). Based on the information about the child's auditory and visual processing strengths and weaknesses, it becomes possible to tailor classroom interventions for each child. The information helps teachers understand the child's processing weaknesses and how to better work with them on academic tasks.

Behavioral Descriptions from the IVA2

The following is a list of the types of behavioral descriptions taken from actual reports to give you an idea of the kinds of processing details obtained from the IVA2 assessment.

- Significant problems remaining alert, likely to tune out
- Problems adapting to changes/transitioning from one activity to another
- Likely to drift off
- Difficulty getting back on track when distracted by auditory or visual stimuli
- Deficits in auditory or visual working memory
- Difficulty in maintaining focus on auditory or visual stimuli
- Difficulty following directions accurately
- Misunderstanding verbal instructions
- Problems with self-esteem or self-confidence
- Erratic responses to auditory or visual stimuli
- Tendency to make more errors when there's a high demand to perform (pressure situations, test taking)
- Frequent lapses in visual or auditory attention
- Rushing through written work, which results in careless errors
- Attention problems related to slow mental processing
- Problems with response inhibition and impulse control tendencies, reflecting carelessness, thoughtlessness, or over-reactivity
- Problems regulating and directing actions when stressed or tired (gives up)
- Acting out, irritability, and negative verbalizations
- Impaired social interactions with peers

- Trouble with self-direction and completing necessary work
- Tendencies reflecting distractible, divergent, or variable attention processing when given a repetitive, demanding, structured, non-entertaining task
- Difficulties learning new tasks in the school environment
- Slow mental processing speed
- Problems sustaining attention and responding consistently when asked questions verbally or given written tests
- Starts tasks then quickly runs out of steam; may be very slow in completing work
- Impulsive, agitated, chaotic, overexcited, and turbulent
- Significant problems with self-control
- Difficulty listening, remembering, or following rules
- Agitated, confused, or excessively impulsive response pattern
- Internally distracted to the point there is difficulty concentrating and performing meaningful mental activities
- Significant trouble with test performance

Parents' Experience of the IVA2 Assessment Results

One of the most touching moments with parents happens during the initial intake process. While their child takes the assessment in a separate room, I continue the intake with parents to understand their concerns and observed behaviors of their child. Their worries are readily evident.

When I review the assessment results with the parents, they're often amazed by how accurately it describes their child. In many instances, the words the parents used just minutes before are repeated back to them from the assessment report. The difference is that now the behaviors are in a context that the parents can better understand.

The behaviors suddenly make sense as parents learn about their child's auditory and visual processing problems. The problems become clearer, but now there's a solution that doesn't involve behavioral modification plans or medications.

The relief and hope parents express changes everything. Not only do they have answers where none existed before, but their child has a way forward to a better life. We also give them interaction tips to support their child during the neurofeedback training process, which allows them to participate (see Chapter 10).

You may recognize your own child in one of the stories that follow.

Success Stories

The following children's stories are included to highlight the various types of conditions and behavioral problems we have improved with neurofeedback. These are brief descriptions of the children at their initial intake, the types of behaviors that were reported, and the subsequent neurofeedback intervention results.

Jayden: "Is Something Wrong with His Brain?"

Jayden's mother was anxious and worried about her nine-year-old son, who described his classmates as "frenemies." She was distraught that he was having such negative social experiences at school. He was a pleasant boy who only wanted to do well, but something was getting in the way. He was easily agitated and frustrated, unable to follow instructions, forgetful, and didn't seem to understand what to do at times. As a result, he started to act out at school and home. When he struggled in school, he would say, "I'm stupid." This was heartbreaking for his mother, who wanted him to take medication to treat his symptoms. Jayden's father (the parents were divorced), who had a medical background, was resistant to medication and concerned about side effects.

The parents were in conflict as to what to do to help their son. Fearing there was "something wrong with his brain," Jayden's mother had arranged for him to undergo multiple types of assessments. After meeting with a local neuropsychologist, they were referred to me.

Our initial assessment revealed that he had significant problems with auditory comprehension, auditory vigilance, and auditory sequential memory. So yes, in some ways, we could say there was something wrong with his brain processing. But neurofeedback could strengthen his neuronal pathways for processing auditory information.

Jayden participated in 20 sessions, and his assessment results were very positive. His extremely impaired auditory comprehension resolved, his auditory vigilance impairment resolved, and his auditory sequential memory improved from 11 percent to 81 percent, all with only 20 sessions of training. A second set of 20 sessions focused on stabilizing these improvements and strengthening his auditory consistency and auditory persistence abilities. The outcome is that medication was avoided, the cause of his difficulties was accurately identified, and his ADHD symptoms were resolved.

Ginny: Anxiety, Learning Disability, and Mild Asperger's Syndrome

Ginny's mother reported that her 17-year-old daughter experienced anxiety, was struggling academically, and had trouble with focus and attention. Ginny would be a senior the next year and needed to attend summer school to improve her grades in English in order to walk at graduation. Her mother felt that Ginny also acted out to get attention from her stepfather, which caused conflict between Ginny and the stepfather.

After neurofeedback, Ginny saw positive results. She was excited that she was able to read a book to completion in just three hours and comprehend it! During her summer school sessions, she received a B in English literature. She also obtained a babysitting job with the goal of saving money for a car. The family for whom she was babysitting commented on her improved ability to focus on multiple things. In regard to her stepfather, she was able to simply walk away when she felt tension building between them. In all, Ginny said her self-awareness improved.

Benjamin: ADHD and ODD

Seven-year-old Benjamin was in constant trouble at school and wouldn't complete his homework. He easily became frustrated and angry. He even got into physical arguments with other students and spat in their faces, resulting in suspension from school.

After neurofeedback, Benjamin said he felt more peaceful and no longer felt the need to spit in people's faces. His mother reported that he was less anxious, more relaxed, and more pleasant to be around.

Eddie: ADHD/ADD and Asperger's Syndrome

Eight-year-old Eddie had difficulty focusing and paying attention in school and was unable to make decisions on his own. He didn't play with other children, preferring to play alone quietly. He had a difficult time with change and repeated words and phrases when he became nervous or agitated.

Toward the end of his neurofeedback program, Eddie's mother reported that her son had begun to relax. At this same time, his primary clinician was out of the office. Prior to neurofeedback, this type of change would have upset him. But his interpersonal skills had improved so much that he spoke to the other clinicians, greeted them, and engaged in appropriate conversations. His mother was surprised and pleased with the changes in her son.

Sara: ADHD

Sara, who was 12 years old, was easily distracted at school. She didn't perform well on tests and was described as hyperactive and unable to focus. She had difficulty completing her homework because she was easily distracted.

After neurofeedback, she started earning As and Bs, which was quite a departure from her prior low grades. She was able to focus and complete her homework successfully. Sara proudly displayed her honor roll certificate, as she had only made the honor roll one other time. Her final assessment results revealed she no longer had ADHD symptoms.

Sydney: ADD/ADHD and Sensory Integration Disorder

Sydney's mother shared that her 11-year-old daughter often became explosive and threw tantrums at home and school. She had been unable to attend school for two months because of the mental and emotional distress. She also had trouble focusing and remembering.

After completing neurofeedback therapy, Sydney was more pleasant to be around. She mellowed out and stopped having tantrums. Her memory also improved, and she was better at focusing and remembering instructions.

Tanisha: ADD

Eight-year-old Tanisha had difficulty with focus and following instructions. In gymnastics, she had to look directly at the coach to be able to understand what he said.

After neurofeedback, she said she was better able to focus and follow verbal instructions without needing to look directly at the person. It was much easier for her to make progress in her gymnastics program, as well as in the classroom.

Toni: ADHD and Anxiety

Toni, age 12, had difficulty paying attention and focusing at school, which led to poor grades. Due to the severity of her anxiety, she constantly bit her nails and picked at her face to the extent that she caused scabs. She was taking ADHD medication.

After neurofeedback, she no longer needed the medication. Her anxiety reduced, she no longer picked at her face, and her scabs resolved. She was mostly earning As and Bs in school, and she could actively participate in class and math tutoring.

Billy: Poor Focus and Attention

Billy, who was seven years old, was struggling in school and had a hard time paying attention in class. As a result, his grades were poor.

After he completed neurofeedback, his tutor and mother shared that he was better able to remain focused during tutoring sessions.

Families and Teachers Describe their Experience of Neurofeedback

While the stories of children's growth are particularly inspiring, we also collected feedback from families and educators about a child's neurofeedback experience. Here are some of their experiences in their own words.

Parent. "My son was part of your neurofeedback program over a year ago. There are not enough words to thank you and your team for all the help you provided him. He was diagnosed with ADD last year, and the only treatment that his pediatrician offered was ADD medicine. We contacted you in hopes of finding an alternative. He received over 20 neurofeedback sessions, and those were the life-changing moment for him and for our family. His change was really amazing. He is now able to focus at school. He is more productive than ever and is able to complete more complex projects. His teacher was surprised with the huge progress he had last academic year. I am a strong supporter of neurofeedback now. Thanks so much for providing such wonderful service to our community."

Parent. "My youngest daughter was late in developing speech. She had been in speech therapy since she was three years old. She had a difficult time cutting with scissors and writing, although she held a pencil correctly. She did not do well in kindergarten. Her IVA2 test results showed she needed much help. Her visual processing was practically nonexistent.

As a parent, I cannot say enough wonderful things about the staff and work of the neurofeedback team. I have recommended neurofeedback to many of my colleagues and friends who have children with special needs or other concerns. Dr. McReynolds and all of the clinicians at her center have encouraged, supported, and helped my youngest daughter with her brain development. Dr. McReynolds gave me suggestions to request from the school that helped my daughter be more successful. As always, she gave me support and encouragement that once again left me hopeful for my youngest daughter's success. Thank you!"

Elementary School Teacher. "Thomas (age eight) had always been sweet and kind, but he would often drift away in the middle of his work. He was so easily distracted. He had difficulty moving from task to task. He had very low work product and low energy. I felt at times that maybe he would just plateau in his progress and that would be it. Then, he started neurofeedback, and everything changed. We would get to the end of the work morning, and he had proudly completed all of his work. I was in shock! I began watching him more closely in class, and sure enough, he was focusing. Then, he started to gain momentum. He was able to take on larger projects and more involved work. At the end, he was confident and a leader in our class. I was amazed."

Reading Teacher. "While I was recovering from surgery, the parent of one of my reading students enrolled her son in neurofeedback with Dr. McReynolds. When I returned to work and engaged again in teaching her son to read, it was very obvious to me that something significant had occurred in his ability to learn. His ability to remember things was the first change I noticed. Then, his ability to absorb what I taught him had clearly improved.

My job at that time was to teach students to read. These students were the ones who did not learn to read in the school setting and had learning disabilities that made it especially difficult for them to master the skill of reading.

Before neurofeedback, I was very concerned that it might take him well into his teenage years to learn to read because he progressed so slowly. After neurofeedback, he was able to progress at a level similar to other children. Later, this child's mom also enrolled her older son in the program because she, too, could see the positive impact on her younger son.

I was so amazed and curious that I enrolled myself. I saw my own improvements and was able to pass the information on to additional parents. In each case where a parent enrolled their child in the program, significant changes occurred that allowed the student to learn with greater ease and efficiency. Neurofeedback is a game-changer for children who struggle to learn."

As we've seen, when the brain is working at more optimal levels, children are able to show their abilities and develop self-confidence. They develop a sense of self-empowerment and begin to believe they're able to handle problems. With these assessments and interventions, everyone wins!

CHAPTER 10

INTERVENTIONS TO EMPOWER YOUR CHILD AT HOME AND SCHOOL

Identifying auditory and visual processing problems for children who struggle with learning and behavior is the first step. As we've discussed, understanding how your child's brain is working (or not working) is crucial to determining how you can support them. When it comes to advocating for school support, you need specific information about your child's auditory and visual processing weaknesses in order to request certain types of classroom interventions. Without this specificity, you won't know what to request to effectively advocate for your child's individual learning, behavioral, or social-emotional needs.

Although each child has a unique set of processing difficulties, we can broadly conceptualize these categories and drill down to their needs. Through the effective identification of auditory and visual processing difficulties, teachers receive concrete information to plan better teaching strategies and instructional techniques. Better assessment data yield better information, and better information yields better understanding and better interventions. In turn, better interventions yield better results for learning.

The following intervention suggestions won't make all the problems of raising children with auditory and visual problems go away, but I've seen them make a substantial difference and ease the stress and anxiety that many children experience.

Tips for Parenting Children with Auditory Processing Problems

To know if your child has auditory processing problems, refer to the checklist at the end of chapter 6 to help you make an informal assessment.

The tips in this and the next section don't require equipment, training manuals, or degrees in child psychology. Yet, they can have a profound impact on your life and your child's life by reducing the stress you both experience.

When implementing these strategies, keep in mind that using a respectful approach is far more helpful to your child than any other approach (such as saying things in a demeaning manner, putting the child down for needing instructions presented in a different way, and so on).

The most important support you can provide is patience. Children with auditory processing difficulties often feel bad about themselves, especially since they may be aware they struggle more than their peers or siblings. Patience and understanding go a long way to help them feel more secure. Sharing these strategies with teachers can also help them better support your child in the classroom.

1. If your child is having difficulty concentrating with background sounds, consider:

    a. providing a quiet space for studying.

    b. reducing background noises by turning off the TV and other devices during homework time.

    c. providing one instruction at a time vs. multiple instructions.

2. Give one instruction, check that your child's understanding of the instruction is accurate, and reinforce the instruction by repeating it. When the task is complete, provide instruction for the second task. Again, check for accuracy, repeat the instruction, and so on.

3. Ask family members to reduce auditory distractions as much as possible during homework time, and use headphones to help with noise reduction.

4. If your child has trouble following longer conversations, break the information into smaller segments to help support the brain's ability to remember information and process it.

5. When your child needs to take notes from verbal information:

    a. Provide smaller amounts of information.

    b. Give them additional time to write down the information.

    c. Repeat the information for improved accuracy.

    d. Assist your child in checking for accuracy.

6. When your child's brain is unable to remember larger segments of information, repeat it and check for accuracy in a kind and empathetic manner.

7. Write down chores and daily tasks in a visible area, and remind your child to check the list.

8. If your child has difficulty maintaining attention when spoken to:

    a. Have them focus on the person who is speaking.

    b. Use the previous approach by breaking information down into smaller segments.

    c. Repeat the information after checking with them for understanding.

9. For some children, spelling and reading are difficult when auditory processing isn't strong enough. To accommodate:

   a. Break the information into smaller segments.

   b. Check with them for understanding.

   c. Repeat the information as needed.

Tips for Parenting Children with Visual Processing Problems

You can use the following approaches to support your child if they have visual processing problems. (Refer to the checklist at the end of chapter 7 to make an informal assessment.)

Again, when implementing these strategies, use a respectful approach. It's also helpful to remember that a child with visual processing problems doesn't know why they're unable to grasp information in the same way as their peers or siblings. This can be a confusing experience for everyone because there are probably some tasks they can do well, while they seem to fall apart on other ones.

1. If your child has difficulty copying or taking notes, if written items are missing words, or if words are missing letters, read the material to them. As you read, always keep in mind how your tone of voice conveys information to your child.

2. When they have difficulty remembering written material that they read silently, switch again to reading the material aloud. Some children with visual processing problems have good auditory functions, and this becomes a viable workaround to accomplish visual tasks.

3. Math skills may be particularly difficult for a child with visual processing problems. Using an alternative approach of reading the material aloud can again be an effective way to support them through difficult academic tasks.

4. If you notice a difference in your child's ability to learn spelling words when studying from a list or using visual study aids, switch to text-to-speech programs on the computer so that they can listen to learn. Text-to-speech functions can assist children with math problems, although some programs are more functional than others.

5. For a child who seems to overlook math signs and posted information:

    a. Use gentle reminders to check their work.

    b. Review their work with them out loud so that they can better understand what they overlook.

    c. Highlight information.

A child with visual processing problems is unable to remember visual information, so asking them to pay attention to what they're looking at tends to be nonproductive. It's a bit like asking a person who writes with their right hand to switch to writing with their left hand and expecting fluency. It just isn't going to be that easy.

Home Intervention—What We Say Matters

There is one technique that isn't frequently discussed, nor is it typically mentioned when parents seek help or when teachers feel challenged in the classroom. Yet, neuroscientists have found that it has the potential to make a significant difference in your child's life and yours as well. It has to do with self-talk, which is defined as what we say to ourselves both out loud and internally.[1] This difference can be positive or negative depending on what's said or thought that expresses a feeling. Some of our self-talk may be helpful, and some of it may not.

Interestingly, when most people are asked what they say to themselves, they rarely have an answer. Yet, I believe self-talk is one of the most important tools to help children develop strong self-confidence and a good sense of self-worth. Scientists have found that when you say something to yourself, either positive or negative, you potentially wire it into your brain, which is similar to the brain processes we've been discussing throughout the book. The more frequently messages are repeated, either by us or others, the more these messages are hardwired into our brain.

After a while, the repeated messages become so ingrained that they're in our subconscious mind (the part of the mind that operates outside of our awareness). The subconscious part of our mind is where our automatic thinking brain resides (autopilot). This is the part of the brain that remembers how to complete tasks like driving a car without consciously thinking about it. This is also the seat of beliefs that either support us or undermine our ability to function and perform in life.[2]

Consider public speaking. Do you enjoy this, or do you steer away from it? It's likely that in either situation, your brain has made the decision for you before you were aware that it did. This is your automatic pilot in action, and it's important to understand how your child may be programming their brain with thoughts and beliefs about their abilities.

To better understand self-talk, let's say you grew up in an average family that was reasonably positive. Even in families like that, research shows that the average child is told "No" or what they can't do more than *148,000* times throughout their childhood.[3] That's a lot of negative feedback! Because the brain processes and remembers repeated messages, this means a child's brain is reinforced negatively 148,000 times. Even in a generally positive family, you may start repeating those words to yourself.

Scientists have also discovered that our brains record *everything* we encounter—*everything* we hear, say, or think! Even more interesting is the discovery that as much as 80 percent of everything a person thinks is negative, counterproductive, and works against them.[4]

And interestingly, about 90 percent of what we think is outside of our awareness. It comes from our subconscious programming that's running on autopilot.[5]

Science has suggested that as much as three-quarters of our automatic thinking isn't helpful. This is particularly important in our discussion of how children learn to perceive themselves, what they say to themselves, and how they feel about themselves.

The neural pathways that are used more increase, and the ones that are used less decrease. So engaging in positive self-talk can override old negative thinking patterns. When you take a positive approach to your own self-talk, as well as your child's problems, you direct your brain and theirs to develop an optimistic outlook. And when we take a positive approach to our problems, we're more likely to have a positive outcome.[6] Simply put, children who have an optimistic outlook have more effective coping skills to handle challenges.

To begin the process of retraining yourself and helping your child train their brain, I recommend the following simple steps. They can make a difference in as little as 30 days.

1. Practice becoming aware of what you are saying to yourself. Since we have so many thoughts throughout the day, you can't possibly be aware of all of them. However, you can redirect any negative thought you catch.

2. Redirect the negative thought to a positive thought. I coach my clients in identifying the negative thought and then saying the exact opposite statement to themselves. At first, your mind will reject the new statement, but with consistent practice and repetition, your mind will begin to work with you instead of against you.

3. At the end of the day before going to sleep, ask your child to identify three things they felt good about during the day. This isn't about what they did well. While that can work, it tends to be a bit judgmental. Instead, focus on three things they felt good

about, such as playing with the family pet, laughing, or feeling happy while playing with friends. Anything goes here as long as it's something they felt good about. Some children may need help to find three things (as will some parents). This practice will help put your child in a positive place as they fall asleep, and it's a nice way to connect positively with them at bedtime.

Switch Up Your Language

You can also work to switch up how you speak to and with your child. Consider what you don't want your child to do. Then, ask them to do what you *do* want them to do. (Remember, if your child has auditory processing problems, you may need to modify your approach.)

For example:

- Instead of saying "don't jump on the sofa," say "please sit on the sofa."
- Instead of saying "don't run through the house," say "please walk through the house."
- Instead of saying, "don't hit your sister," say "please touch your sister gently."
- Instead of saying "don't throw your toys on the floor," say "please put your toys away gently."
- Instead of saying "don't shout in the house," say "use your quiet voice in the house."

These simple changes may not seem like much, but given the research on how many times a child hears "no" or "don't do that," changing your language can be a more positive way to interact with your child. Communication simply works best when we ask for what we want instead of saying what we don't want. This will help your child learn how to ask for what they need as well. Both of you will learn through this process.

Equipped with this information, you can make a conscious decision with each interaction about what you want to develop in your child's brain. Is it a positive message?

Positive thinking leads to lasting changes and a willingness to learn. Don't skip it, as it's an integral part of addressing your child's behaviors and learning needs.

School Services That Can Help Your Child

Over the past decade of working with parents of children who struggle in school, many have been unaware of their legal rights to educational support for their children. The following sections provide a brief review of Section 504 of the Rehabilitation Act, the Individualized Educational Plan (IEP) process, and the Individual Service Plan (for private schools; see Appendix D for a comparison chart).

General education school interventions fall into one of three categories: academic support, behavioral support, or social-emotional support. It's critical to understand that all of these interventions rely on a child being able to process auditory and visual information.

Section 504 of the Rehabilitation Act

Section 504 of the Rehabilitation Act of 1973 is a federal law protecting the rights of individuals with disabilities in the general educational setting. If your child continues to struggle with educational challenges and is believed to need additional academic services, they can be considered for special education evaluations or related services. These help identify disabilities that impact your child's ability to learn, and help determine which program is appropriate to meet their educational needs.

Section 504 is part of the federal civil rights law ensuring all children within the education system, regardless of their disabilities, have equal guaranteed access to an education. Unlike an IEP (see the next section), a full assessment isn't required for 504 accommodations.

At the general education academic level, a 504 plan supports your child's learning through school-based accommodations like extra test time, the use of audiobooks, speech-to-text software, or the option to type writing assignments.[7]

To obtain the most appropriate accommodations, parents are recommended to work with their child's school personnel to develop the 504 plan and ensure all who work with the child are aware of it and agree with it.

To implement a 504 plan, you have the right as a parent to request a meeting through the school administrator or 504 coordinator to discuss accommodations to best meet the academic needs of your child. Each school district has its own process and documentation requirements, however. In most schools, a meeting is held to discuss how the 504 plan could benefit the child in and outside the classroom. The plan will specify accommodations, and at the end of the year, it may be reviewed.

Accommodations can be for the classroom and for unstructured time such as recess and on the bus, as well as for transitions to and from various settings. Accommodations can include test modifications, organization and behavioral management, and the physical arrangement of the classroom. Once the team agrees, the plan is provided to all members, including noon-duty aids and substitute teachers, to ensure the accommodations are offered. The 504 plan is considered a legal plan and follows your child into the next school year.

If there are still concerns after the 504 plan has been in place for at least six weeks, the team can revisit it. If the accommodations aren't working, the team can recommend further assessments.

Individual Educational Plan (IEP)

IEP stands for *Individualized Education Program* or *Individualized Education Plan,* which are used interchangeably. The IEP is a legally binding document that identifies the type of special education services your child will receive, such as having a one-on-one aide in the classroom, setting academic and behavioral goals, and how much time will be spent in both general and special education settings. It includes progress reports from teachers and support providers. The IEP is established at a meeting involving parents/guardians and relevant staff such as the teacher, administrator, intervention specialist, and school psychologist.[8]

Based on your child's abilities and needs, recommendations will be made for academic interventions or for a referral for additional assessments such as a psychoeducational assessment, which includes documentation referred to as the "Assessment Plan." Rating scales are included from parents/guardians that provide insight from their perspective on how their child is functioning at home.

Once the IEP has been signed, the team has 60 days to complete the assessments, which depend on the needs of your child. They may include academic, cognitive, observational, and behavioral/social-emotional assessments. The process can also include additional related services of speech and language, occupational therapy, and mental health assessments. At the end of the 60-day assessment process, an IEP meeting will take place with the team to review the assessment information and determine eligibility. The team meeting will include administrator(s), teacher(s), parent(s)/guardian(s), and school psychologist(s).

Criteria for an IEP falls within 13 areas of eligibility: Autism, Intellectual Disability (ID), Other Health Impaired (OHI), Specific Learning Disability (SLD), Emotional Disturbance (ED), Visual Impairment (VI), Hearing Impairment (HI), Multiple Disabilities, Orthopedic Impairment, Deafness, Deafness and Blindness, Traumatic Brain Injury (TBI), and Speech and Language disorder. Children with ADHD may meet the criteria for "Other Health Impaired."

If your child doesn't qualify in any of the 13 areas, they may still be considered for a 504 plan. Eligibility is based on meeting certain criteria that impacts academic growth. It isn't a diagnosis, but can be used as supporting documentation for a medical professional to consider. A medical professional's diagnosis and recommendations are considered in the development of an IEP (and a 504 plan), but it doesn't guarantee the issuance of an IEP plan.

Once an IEP is developed, it will include annual goals tailored to your child's academic, behavioral, or social-emotional needs for the next academic year. Progress toward those goals will be sent with grades at the end of the quarter or semester. A full psychological evaluation will be done every three years, while goals will be reviewed at the annual meeting.

The IEP and 504 plans are legal documents that are designed to ensure that the school provides the correct accommodations, goals, and modifications to help your child succeed in school.

Individual Service Plan (ISP)

For parents whose child is attending a private school, the IEP and 504 plans do not apply. Instead, private schools may implement an Individual Service Plan. (See Appendix D for a comparison between IEPs, 504 plans, and ISPs.)

For parents seeking additional school-based support, providing schools with a copy of the IVA2 assessment has been an effective way to advocate for specific and individualized academic assistance. The IVA2 assessment provides educators with the identified areas of weaknesses in auditory and visual processing abilities that are affecting your child's ability to perform well academically.

For more information on school-based educational support plans, please see the Resources section.

CHAPTER II

INTERVENTIONS FOR TEACHERS TO HELP THEIR STUDENTS

Teachers often struggle to help students with processing problems because they focus on the disruptive behaviors or assume the students have learning disabilities. When they understand that behaviors are a form of communication, educators are better able to provide needed support. Focusing solely on eliminating disruptive behaviors places the emphasis on the wrong problem. Yes, disruptive behaviors must be addressed, but without understanding the cause of the behaviors, the interventions may be off the mark in helping the child achieve self-regulation.

In addition, many traditional school-based assessments are administered to children who are struggling with auditory and visual processing problems. If your child has one or both of these processing difficulties, the assessment results may misidentify their learning problems.

The Limits of Traditional School-Based Assessments: Brittney's Story

By design, school assessments attempt to identify academic problems in struggling children. But assessments that require auditory and visual processing may lead to poor testing results for a child who lacks these processing abilities and have the potential to miss the mark on the actual cause of the child's learning difficulties.

Brittney is one such child who faced the limits of the traditional approach. She came to us after her grandmother learned of our intervention services and requested that I participate in Brittney's IEP (Individualized Educational Plan) meeting to support her parents, who were struggling with an unwanted label from the school.

Brittney was in the sixth grade and unable to read. She struggled with spelling, speech abilities, and math. The school district had assessed her using the standardized testing approach and concluded she was in the mild/moderate intellectual disabilities range with speech and language difficulties. Because of Brittany's functional abilities at home, her parents disagreed with the mild/moderate intellectual disabilities label and countered the school's interpretation.

Brittney took the IVA2 assessment as part of our intake process, which revealed she didn't have *any* visual processing abilities and had mixed auditory processing abilities. Any child without visual processing abilities will feel lost in the classroom, be unable to follow along with visual tasks, unable to attend to classroom presentations, and look lost or inattentive. Her auditory processing abilities were also what I have dubbed a "Swiss cheese pattern" of functioning. She had some auditory processing abilities, but they weren't strong across all assessed areas. Some areas worked; others did not.

Attending the IEP meeting online was a disheartening process. After listening to school personnel for 40 minutes while they exhaustively identified Brittney's extremely low scores on all of her academic assessments, with only one aspect of functioning in social behaviors that was in the "normal" range, Brittney's parents were deflated. The educational psychologist suggested that she had a cognitive disability, which raised a question in my mind, as no cognitive assessment results had been reported.

Based on my assessment results, Brittney had extremely impaired visual processing. Once again, she had a *processing* problem, which has to do with sequencing and comprehending information. It may not be due to a cognitive limitation. As we've discussed throughout these pages, children can be in the normal range of intelligence, but unable to demonstrate their abilities because of weak neural pathways in the brain.

After listening to the school personnel, I felt it was important to help the parents and teachers better understand what was happening with Brittney. She had the unfortunate combination of auditory and visual processing problems that makes a classroom setting almost a perfect storm of interference in not supporting her learning needs. Too much visual distraction and too many auditory distractions, coupled with significant sequencing problems, meant she was unable to benefit from the traditional learning environment or from traditional academic interventions.

Sequencing problems interrupted her ability to put things in the correct order, and when combined with her spotty auditory processing abilities, she was at an extreme disadvantage in the traditional school setting. The deck was stacked against her through no fault of her own or anyone else's. The academic system simply isn't set up to help a child with this combination of processing problems. They generally don't have the assessment tools or the intervention processes specific enough to help the Brittney's of the world.

Her visual processing problems negatively affected her ability to write or perform sequenced spelling tasks because she was unable to put tasks and steps in the correct order. Her auditory processing weaknesses meant she was catching one or two words out of every ten that were spoken to her. When coupled with her extremely impaired auditory sequencing, she just couldn't remember or follow step-by-step instructions. She was perpetually lost in the classroom setting. And even worse, since she was ending the sixth grade, the school had recommended that she be placed in the moderate/severe intellectually disabled category as she entered middle school. In my opinion, this was an incorrect and inappropriate approach, and her parents were committed to avoiding it at all costs.

To help Brittney and help the school to meet her needs, I recommended the following interventions: (1) extend her accommodations to include one-on-one classroom instruction to address her sequencing, as well as visual and auditory problems; (2) include auditory comprehension checks when presenting visual tasks; and (3) for the speech and language interventions, move her to one-on-one instructions instead of placing her in a group learning setting, which was far too disruptive because of her visual and auditory distractibility.

We provided 20 sessions of neurofeedback training for Brittney. Interestingly, her working memory score (short-term memory ability) improved from zero percent on her initial assessment to 88 percent, which is a passing score. This was a clear indication that she responded well to the neurofeedback interventions. Her parents were pleased with her progress and continued to advocate for improved services and support in the school setting.

In many ways, Brittney was being blamed for not being able to learn. In this case, because the school was uncertain about the actual cause of her learning problems, they were ready to label her as intellectually delayed.

We can and must do better. Far too much is at stake when even one child is misdiagnosed based on a misunderstanding of the cause of the problem. Children who fall into these categories at school may be cast into a trajectory from which they can't easily emerge. When children are misclassified, their abilities, talents, and skills can be overlooked, while their self-esteem and self-confidence may be inadvertently diminished. Thankfully, we now have the tools to help schools and educators in new ways.

What Teachers and Schools Can Do

Teachers who are aware of how students learn (or don't learn) are better equipped to implement effective and specific classroom-based interventions. When students with learning difficulties have trouble keeping up, teachers need to be able to identify and implement interventions and support in the classroom to help students meet grade-level performance expectations.

Each school offers different interventions to support students in reading, writing, and math. Supports and interventions can be implemented in and out of the classroom by the teacher or paraprofessionals, and academic progress can be monitored.

Depending on the level of additional supports your child may need, services may include:

- one-on-one classroom supports
- home instruction
- extra time for homework or tests
- extra check-ins from teachers
- access to electronic devices (such as laptops equipped with voice-to-text features)

Parents can request these types of academic supports through a 504 plan or an IEP (see the previous chapter for more details).

Regardless of whether you opt to implement a formal process— like a 504 plan, IEP, or ISP—there are numerous ways for teachers to support children in their classrooms. Similar to the lists of ways for parents to support children with auditory and visual processing problems, the next sections outline various interventions that teachers can use to empower children in the general education setting.

It bears repeating that children with auditory and visual processing problems need a great deal of empathy and kindness. Far too many children with these problems have been treated harshly, heavily punished, and even suffered abuse. Children with these problems aren't the *cause* of their problems, and they don't understand why they're in trouble so often. They need supportive and nurturing interventions to help them grow and flourish.

Tips for Teachers of Children with Auditory Processing Problems

Here are ways that teachers can support children who are having difficulty with auditory processing:[1]

1. Reduce background noise, when possible.
2. Seat the student near the teacher and away from auditory distractions, such as doors and windows.
3. Speak clearly and slowly when presenting new information.
4. Provide a quiet area for test-taking or to work on assignments away from distractions.
5. Provide a quiet area for independent work.
6. Check in frequently to make sure the student understands the work assignment.

When giving verbal instructions in the classroom:

1. Give step-by-step instructions, and have the student repeat them back to you.
2. Use attention-getting phrases like: "This is important to know because . . ."
3. Decide with the student on a nonverbal signal to show that a key point is being made.
4. Say directions, assignments, and schedules out loud, and rephrase as needed.

5. Repeat key information throughout the lesson, and rephrase as needed.

6. Use visual tools, images, and gestures to enhance and support spoken lessons.

7. Break down test or classwork instructions into short, written steps.

8. Highlight key words and ideas on worksheets.

For completing tests and assignments, consider the following:

1. Give written homework instructions.

2. Provide a list of homework assignments for the week or day.

3. Give material on a new concept to the student before it's taught to the whole class so that the student can get familiar with it ahead of time.

4. Give a list of (or highlight) key vocabulary and concepts for upcoming lessons.

5. Give a short review or connection to a previous lesson before teaching something new.

6. Give the student an outline of the lesson.

7. Grade based on the student's completion of the lesson goal. For instance, don't grade spelling errors if that isn't the focus of the lesson.

Tips for Teachers of Children with Visual Processing Problems

The following are ways teachers can support children who are having difficulties with visual processing:[2]

1. Read visual schedules and written instructions aloud.

2. Describe visual presentations verbally or provide narration.

3. Build in time to summarize the important information from each lesson.

4. Provide uncluttered handouts with few or no nonessential images.

5. Use a reading guide strip or a blank index card to block out other lines of text while reading.

6. Provide a highlighter for highlighting information while reading.

7. Highlight math symbols.

8. Provide a slant board (or three-ring binder) to bring work closer to the student's visual field.

9. Provide wide-ruled paper, and darken or highlight lines and margins to help form letters in the right space.

10. Provide graph paper to help line up math problems.

11. Provide a note-taker or a copy of class notes.

12. Allow the student to use different-colored pencils, pens, and/or highlighters.

When giving visual instructions in the classroom:

1. Clearly space words and problems on the page.

2. Write directions in a different color from the rest of an assignment, or highlight them.

3. Say directions and assignments out loud.

4. Include simple diagrams or images to clarify written directions.

5. Check in and allow time for the student to ask questions about directions.

For completing tests and assignments, consider the following:

1. Allow verbal reporting instead of written responses.

2. Allow the student to submit answers on a separate sheet of paper rather than fitting them into small spaces.

3. Reduce visual distractions by folding a test or using blank pieces of paper to cover up part of the page.

4. Provide extended time on tests.

5. Provide a quiet room for tests if needed.

.

CHAPTER 12

THE ELEMENTARY SCHOOL PILOT PROJECT

Co-authored by Cynthia Britt, Ph.D.

After years of development, I was granted permission to set up a neurofeedback system in an elementary school with the goal of providing in-school services to children who were struggling in the classroom. Based on the results I'd seen in my clinics, I wanted to expand beyond the clinical setting to show how neurofeedback can help children, parents, and educators in schools.

It was my belief that working with educators in a school-based setting would allow more children to be served during the school day by lessening the distance and time parents need to travel to get services. In addition, there would be an opportunity for educators to learn more about the daily impact of auditory and visual processing problems. The neurofeedback assessments and interventions were used in addition to the school-based interventions for children at risk of referral to special education.[1] These were children who hadn't responded to traditional school-based interventions for academic and behavioral concerns.

There were many rewarding parts of this program, not the least of which was helping teachers better understand the classroom behaviors of troubled or inattentive children. In some cases, the child's teacher was involved in the review of the assessment during the intake with the parents. It was during these meetings that I witnessed a change in how the teacher perceived the behaviors of the child. It was a game-changer when they saw definitive information identifying auditory and visual processing weaknesses and understood how these weaknesses affected the child's ability to function, learn, attend, sit still, concentrate, and remember information.

This enabled them to develop child-specific classroom interventions and supports by identifying ways to help the child manage their auditory and visual processing challenges while attending neurofeedback sessions.

As the sessions progressed, the school psychologist was in regular communication with the teachers and parents about classroom and home supports. During the first 20 sessions, teachers and parents began to see noticeable differences in the children's abilities to remain focused and attentive.[2]

Their success, as illustrated in the examples and testimonials that follow demonstrate the value of embedding neurofeedback programs within the school setting. The upcoming sections present the assessments and outcomes of three children who participated in the pilot project, along with testimonials from the staff, administrators, and children who participated.[3]

Student Stories

Timmy (Age 7)

Timmy's initial assessment revealed he had extremely impaired visual processing abilities, which had a significant effect on his ability to pay attention when his teacher was writing on the whiteboard or when he took notes, did math, or wrote spelling words. Although his auditory processing abilities were stronger than his visual abilities, he still had significant difficulties in some areas of auditory processing, which made it hard to pay attention when his teacher was speaking. He had trouble remembering what he was supposed to do or how to complete a project. (The Invalid notation on the graph is interpreted as a zero score, but it doesn't mean the assessment was invalid.)

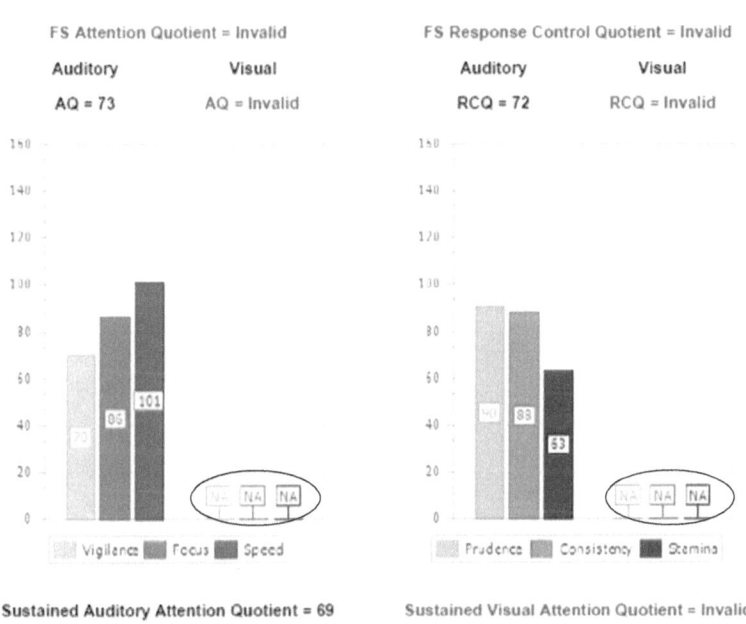

FS Attention Quotient = Invalid

Auditory   Visual

AQ = 73   AQ = Invalid

FS Response Control Quotient = Invalid

Auditory   Visual

RCQ = 72   RCQ = Invalid

Sustained Auditory Attention Quotient = 69   Sustained Visual Attention Quotient = Invalid

Timmy also had moderately impaired fine motor hyperactivity, extremely impaired visual comprehension, severely impaired visual persistence, and mildly impaired visual sensory motor abilities, as seen in the next graph.

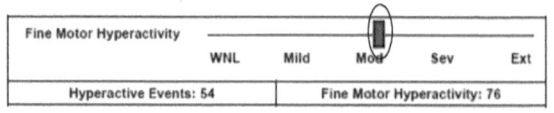

Fine Motor Hyperactivity		WNL	Mild	Mod	Sev	Ext
Hyperactive Events: 54			Fine Motor Hyperactivity: 76			

Symptomatic	Raw	Quotient	WNL	Mild	Mod	Sev	Ext
Comprehension (A)	93.8%	94	▮				
Comprehension (V)	49.3%	10					▮
Persistence (A)	93.8%	101	▮				
Persistence (V)	60.4%	74				▮	
Sensory/Motor (A)	313 ms	102	▮				
Sensory/Motor (V)	311 ms	84			▮		

To understand how these weaknesses affected Timmy, his impaired fine motor hyperactivity measured his off-task behaviors, meaning it was difficult for him to remain on-task without prompts. His impaired visual comprehension affected his ability to understand visual instructions. His impaired visual persistence made it hard for him to complete visual tasks such as correctly writing spelling words, copying information, and reading. His impaired visual sensory motor abilities meant he had a slower reaction time that could negatively affect his ability to perform well on tests. In the classroom, he had trouble remaining in his seat, paying attention to activities, paying attention when reading, and maintaining attention to complete his work.

Before the neurofeedback intervention, Timmy's teachers were concerned about his poor attention. They reported it was hard for him to do work at grade level or make academic progress even with interventions. His math and writing grades were affected because he lacked attention to detail, and he was overwhelmed. As a result, he was failing and had been referred to special education for assessment. All previous school interventions, which relied on his ability to process auditory and visual information, hadn't brought about lasting behavioral changes or improved his grades.

In my opinion, Timmy's identified auditory and visual processing weaknesses contributed to his lack of success with the traditional interventions because they relied so heavily on the skills he lacked. As noted earlier, these impairments can also limit the accuracy and effectiveness of some assessments because most of them rely on the child's ability to process auditory and visual information.

Timmy's Second Assessment

After 20 sessions of neurofeedback, Timmy's reassessment showed a significant improvement in his visual and auditory processing scores. The initial assessment graph is below, and the reassessment graph is on the following page. He demonstrated substantial improvement in visual vigilance, visual focus, visual speed, visual prudence, visual consistency, and visual stamina—all of which were initially assessed as invalid (zero). In addition, his auditory vigilance, auditory prudence, and auditory stamina improved.

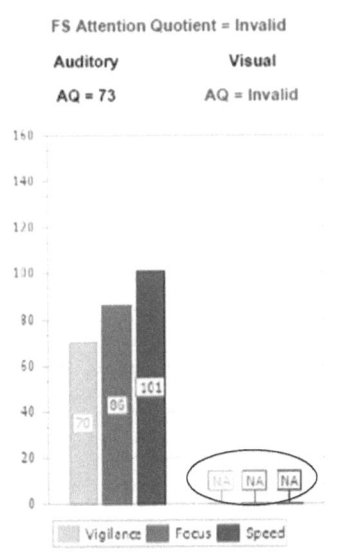

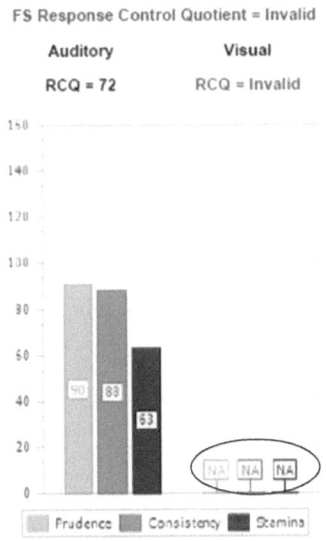

Sustained Auditory Attention Quotient = 69   Sustained Visual Attention Quotient = Invalid

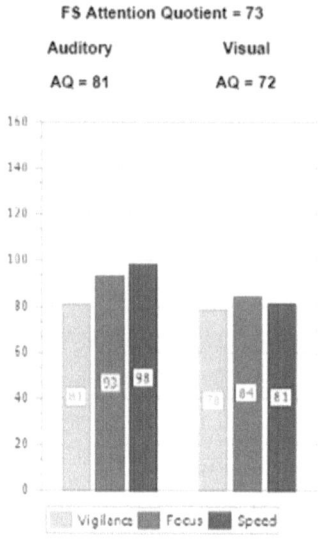

FS Attention Quotient = 73

Auditory	Visual
AQ = 81	AQ = 72

Vigilance Focus Speed

Sustained Auditory Attention Quotient = 50

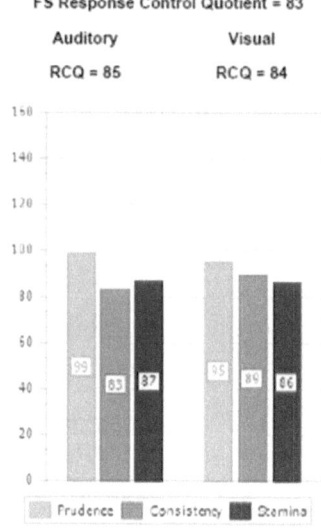

FS Response Control Quotient = 83

Auditory	Visual
RCQ = 85	RCQ = 84

Prudence Consistency Stamina

Sustained Visual Attention Quotient = 61

On the reassessment, (see graph on the next page) improvements were also seen in Timmy's fine motor hyperactivity, his visual persistence, and visual sensory-motor abilities. (His initial graph is below.)

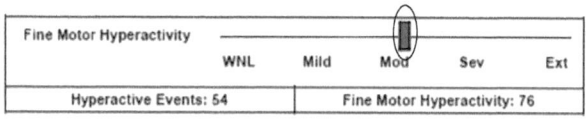

Fine Motor Hyperactivity					
	WNL	Mild	Mod	Sev	Ext
Hyperactive Events: 54		Fine Motor Hyperactivity: 76			

Symptomatic	Raw	Quotient	WNL	Mild	Mod	Sev	Ext
Comprehension (A)	93.8%	94					
Comprehension (V)	49.3%	10					
Persistence (A)	93.8%	101					
Persistence (V)	60.4%	74					
Sensory/Motor (A)	313 ms	102					
Sensory/Motor (V)	311 ms	84					

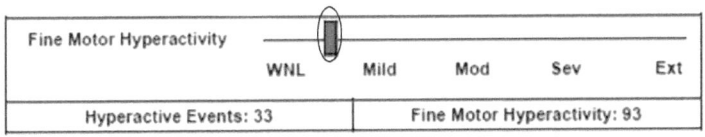

		WNL	Mild	Mod	Sev	Ext
Fine Motor Hyperactivity						

Hyperactive Events: 33	Fine Motor Hyperactivity: 93

Symptomatic	Raw	Quotient	WNL	Mild	Mod	Sev	Ext
Comprehension (A)	80.0%	46					
Comprehension (V)	77.1%	69					
Persistence (A)	65.9%	88					
Persistence (V)	79.6%	87					
Sensory/Motor (A)	271 ms	110					
Sensory/Motor (V)	264 ms	104					

Timmy's teacher reported that he was performing academic tasks and reading closer to his grade level, his on-task behaviors had improved, and he was more willing to participate in classroom activities.

Even with the significant improvements seen across many areas of processing, Timmy continued to struggle with comprehending both auditory and visual information. Two areas of auditory comprehension and auditory persistence showed a decline in abilities. This isn't an uncommon occurrence due to the number of changes he accomplished across so many areas. Training the brain isn't a linear process, so children who achieve noteworthy changes in some areas may temporarily decline in others.

Typically, we would engage a child like Timmy in another 20 sessions of neurofeedback to strengthen these remaining areas. However, this wasn't possible due to the interruption of the pandemic. On the positive side, Timmy's academic performance had improved to such a level that he no longer needed a referral to special education, which was another goal of the program.

Andrea (Age 7)

Andrea's initial assessment (see graph below) revealed she was extremely impaired in visual processing in the areas of vigilance, focus, speed, prudence, consistency, and stamina. She had mostly average scores for auditory processing but was severely impaired in auditory comprehension and extremely impaired in visual comprehension (see graph on the following page).

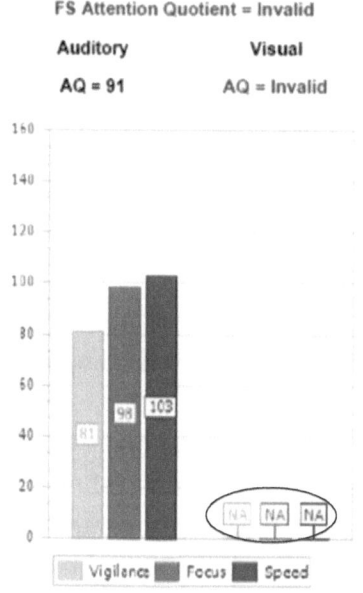
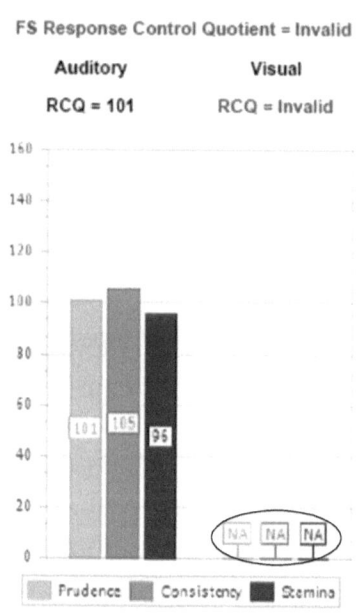

Sustained Auditory Attention Quotient = 74   Sustained Visual Attention Quotient = Invalid

These scores meant she was struggling with information provided visually. In the classroom, this caused difficulties with accurately copying words or letters, taking notes, or leaving out words or letters when writing.

Andrea was very emotionally unregulated with frequent meltdowns at home, she was unable to organize her schoolwork, she couldn't remember what she'd been shown or told, and she had poor self-control.

At school, she was "flying under the radar" by hiding from interactions in the classroom. She was withdrawn and socially isolated with few friends. Academically, she was able to perform at grade level but was still struggling. If she made a mistake, she quietly broke down emotionally in the classroom because she felt embarrassed by how she was performing. But because she was so withdrawn, she wasn't a distraction in the classroom.

The school provided a speech-to-text accommodation to help her express her thoughts, which supported her in a meaningful way and helped reduce her emotional breakdowns in the classroom.

The graph below reflects Andrea's severely and extremely impaired scores in auditory and visual comprehension.

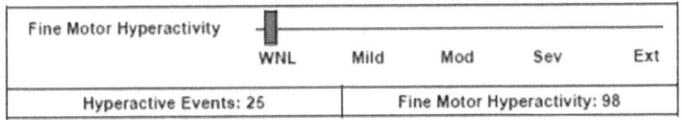

Fine Motor Hyperactivity						
	WNL	Mild	Mod	Sev	Ext	
Hyperactive Events: 25			Fine Motor Hyperactivity: 98			

Symptomatic	Raw	Quotient	WNL	Mild	Mod	Sev	Ext
Comprehension (A)	86.9%	70					
Comprehension (V)	76.4%	52					
Persistence (A)	99.9%	102					
Persistence (V)	125.3%	106					
Sensory/Motor (A)	270 ms	114					
Sensory/Motor (V)	290 ms	107					

Andrea's impaired comprehension created difficulty with math. Her assessment results helped her teacher understand her classroom struggles. The specific auditory and visual processing information assisted the teacher in developing an individualized approach that included checking in to verify she understood the assignment and supplementing visual instructions with verbal instructions. Each of these learning modifications were improvements for Andrea.

After 20 sessions of neurofeedback, Andrea's reassessment (see Appendix F for her report) showed significant improvement in visual processing, as seen in the graph on the next page. (Her initial assessment is below.) Her previous invalid/zero scores for all areas of visual processing were now measurable, and her visual prudence and visual stamina scores were in the average range.

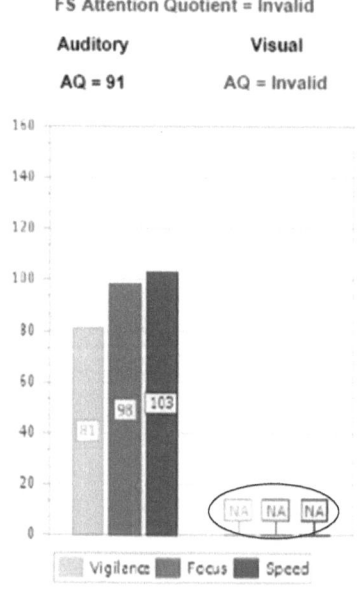

Sustained Auditory Attention Quotient = 74

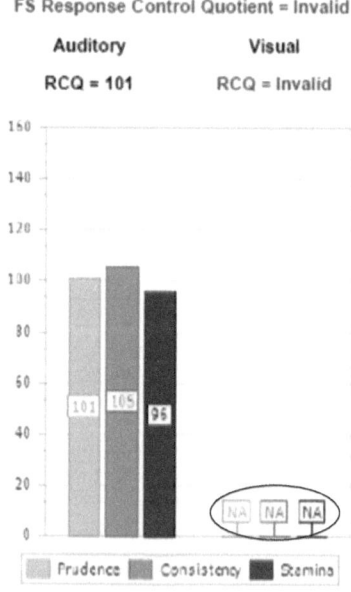

Sustained Visual Attention Quotient = Invalid

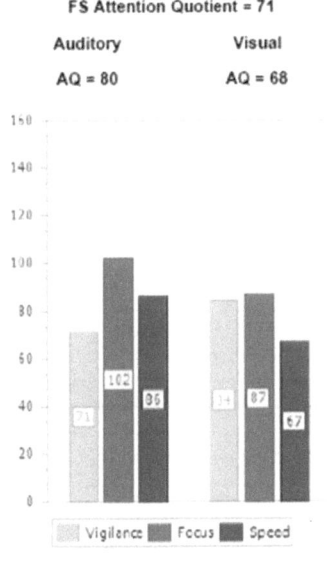

FS Attention Quotient = 71

Auditory	Visual
AQ = 80	AQ = 68

Vigilance · Focus · Speed

Sustained Auditory Attention Quotient = 60

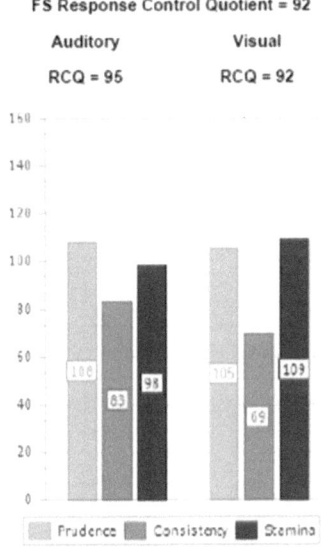

FS Response Control Quotient = 92

Auditory	Visual
RCQ = 95	RCQ = 92

Prudence · Consistency · Stamina

Sustained Visual Attention Quotient = 63

Andrea also had improvements in her visual comprehension, which improved from the extremely impaired range to mildly impaired, as seen in the graph on the next page. (Her initial graph is below.)

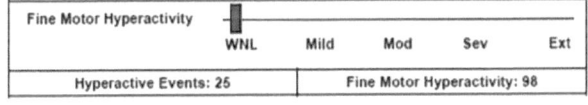

			WNL	Mild	Mod	Sev	Ext
Fine Motor Hyperactivity							

Hyperactive Events: 25	Fine Motor Hyperactivity: 98

Symptomatic	Raw	Quotient	WNL	Mild	Mod	Sev	Ext
Comprehension (A)	86.9%	70					
Comprehension (V)	76.4%	52					
Persistence (A)	99.9%	102					
Persistence (V)	125.3%	106					
Sensory/Motor (A)	270 ms	114					
Sensory/Motor (V)	290 ms	107					

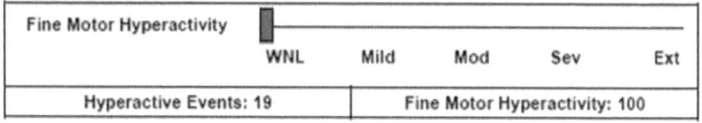

			WNL	Mild	Mod	Sev		Ext
Fine Motor Hyperactivity								

Hyperactive Events: 19	Fine Motor Hyperactivity: 100

Symptomatic	Raw	Quotient	WNL	Mild	Mod	Sev	Ext
Comprehension (A)	85.4%	52					
Comprehension (V)	90.0%	83					
Persistence (A)	72.5%	89					
Persistence (V)	77.9%	91					
Sensory/Motor (A)	260 ms	114					
Sensory/Motor (V)	274 ms	102					

In functional terms, Andrea was able to better understand and process visual information. Due to the neurofeedback intervention, she remained in the general education classroom and no longer needed a referral to special education.

Ideally, we would have provided an additional 20 sessions of neurofeedback to strengthen Andrea's remaining weaknesses, but this was again interrupted due to the onset of the pandemic and school closure. Based on my work with other children, I believe that an additional 20 sessions would have improved Andrea's remaining areas of weakness.

Amanda (Age 6)

With Amanda, we found that both areas of processing were in the extremely impaired range. All of her initial scores were zero. These results meant Amanda had great difficulty processing both auditory and visual information and was at risk for being mistakenly identified as having a cognitive delay.

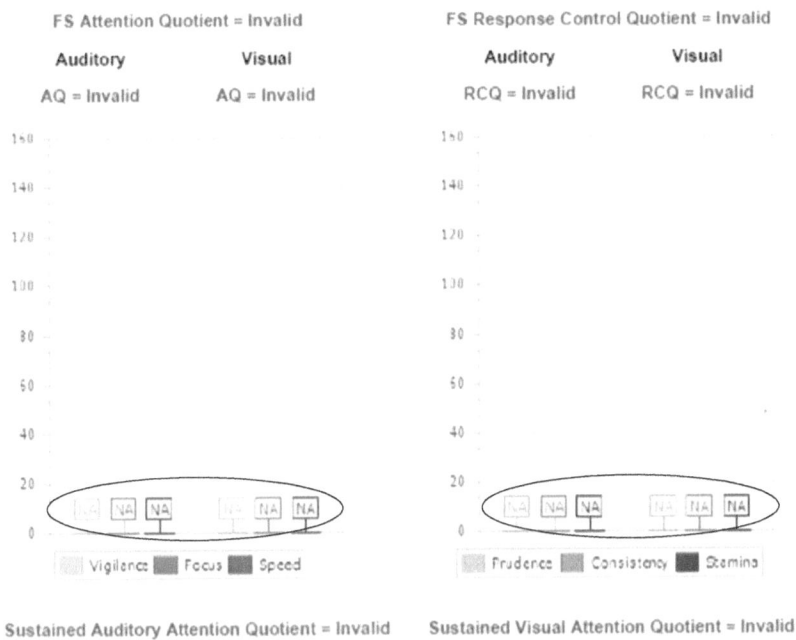

FS Attention Quotient = Invalid

Auditory   Visual

AQ = Invalid   AQ = Invalid

Vigilance Focus Speed

Sustained Auditory Attention Quotient = Invalid

FS Response Control Quotient = Invalid

Auditory   Visual

RCQ = Invalid   RCQ = Invalid

Prudence Consistency Stamina

Sustained Visual Attention Quotient = Invalid

Amanda had a lot of unregulated behaviors. She talked out loud incessantly, didn't complete or turn in her homework, frequently spoke out of turn, and regularly got out of her seat. She was consistently in conflict with her peers and was disorganized and unable to manage paperwork. She struggled with attendance and had difficulty reading.

Children with both auditory and visual processing weaknesses like Amanda usually have trouble learning in a general education classroom and are referred for special education services. To determine special education supports, the required assessments rely on their ability to process auditory and visual communication, which, as we've discussed, can be problematic. So children like Amanda may be at the greatest risk of unnecessary placement in special education.

The following graphs reflect Amanda's extremely impaired auditory and visual comprehension abilities.

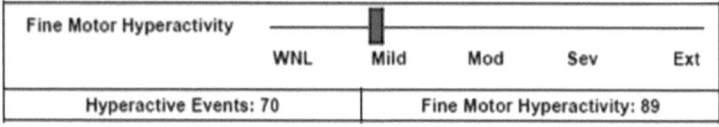

Fine Motor Hyperactivity					
	WNL	Mild	Mod	Sev	Ext

Hyperactive Events: 70	Fine Motor Hyperactivity: 89

Symptomatic	Raw	Quotient	WNL	Mild	Mod	Sev	Ext
Comprehension (A)	70.8%	36					
Comprehension (V)	61.4%	53					
Persistence (A)	73.7%	89					
Persistence (V)	86.8%	92					
Sensory/Motor (A)	365 ms	103					
Sensory/Motor (V)	347 ms	92					

When these assessment results were shared with her team of educators and her parents, it was an eye-opening experience for everyone. Suddenly, it was possible to understand why she had such a hard time learning. She was unable to comprehend auditory and visual information across many areas.

As seen on Amanda's reassessment graph (see second graph on the next page), her auditory and visual processing scores improved significantly after 20 sessions of neurofeedback therapy. She had measurable scores for each of the auditory and visual measures, and all of her scores were in the average range and above average range except her visual vigilance score. (Her initial assessment is at the top of the next page.)

FS Attention Quotient = Invalid

Auditory	Visual
AQ = Invalid	AQ = Invalid

FS Response Control Quotient = Invalid

Auditory	Visual
RCQ = Invalid	RCQ = Invalid

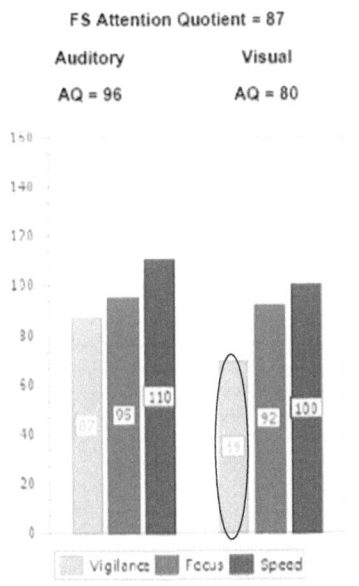

Sustained Auditory Attention Quotient = Invalid

Sustained Visual Attention Quotient = Invalid

FS Attention Quotient = 87

Auditory	Visual
AQ = 96	AQ = 80

FS Response Control Quotient = 106

Auditory	Visual
RCQ = 106	RCQ = 105

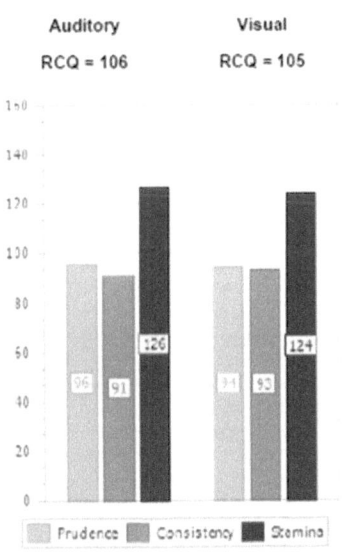

Sustained Auditory Attention Quotient = 89

Sustained Visual Attention Quotient = 83

As you can see in the second graph below, her auditory and visual comprehension scores shifted to the average range, and her mild fine motor hyperactivity shifted toward the average range. (Her initial graph is immediately below.)

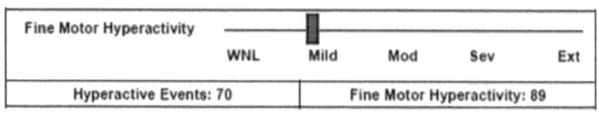

		WNL	Mild	Mod	Sev	Ext
Fine Motor Hyperactivity						

Hyperactive Events: 70	Fine Motor Hyperactivity: 89

Symptomatic	Raw	Quotient	WNL	Mild	Mod	Sev	Ext
Comprehension (A)	70.8%	36					
Comprehension (V)	61.4%	53					
Persistence (A)	73.7%	89					
Persistence (V)	86.8%	92					
Sensory/Motor (A)	365 ms	103					
Sensory/Motor (V)	347 ms	92					

		WNL	Mild	Mod	Sev	Ext
Fine Motor Hyperactivity						

Hyperactive Events: 31	Fine Motor Hyperactivity: 92

Symptomatic	Raw	Quotient	WNL	Mild	Mod	Sev	Ext
Comprehension (A)	93.1%	91					
Comprehension (V)	93.6%	101					
Persistence (A)	94.5%	100					
Persistence (V)	96.9%	96					
Sensory/Motor (A)	433 ms	94					
Sensory/Motor (V)	321 ms	100					

These results were exciting. Where we previously had seen difficulties in Amanda's auditory and visual processing, she was now able to function better in life and school. Most importantly, her teachers reported positive changes in her classroom behaviors and academic achievement. She was able to follow along and wait her turn to speak. She was able to complete and turn in her homework, and she managed her peer relationships more effectively. Her teachers noted that her self-confidence had improved, and she needed fewer behavioral interventions. There were no additional requests for a special education referral.

Families, Teachers, and School Officials Describe Their Experiences

The neurofeedback pilot program included information from teachers, families, the school psychologist, and school administrators about how the children performed both academically and behaviorally.[4] Here are some of their responses:

Grandparent:
"As a grandfather, I saw a great improvement in my grandson's behavior. He was more willing to follow the rules or at least admit when he was wrong. Improvement in his behavior was also evident in the classroom, and he was seen less in the office for behavioral interventions. I would like to obtain more of the neurofeedback services for my grandson when the program resumes."

Parent:
"My son always struggled with his behaviors. After attending the school's neurofeedback program, my son was doing so well in containing himself better. The program helped him so much."

Parent:
"My daughter participated in the school's neurofeedback program. Based on her success, I hope to be able to get this program for her again when we are back at the school. The program was interrupted due to the pandemic. My other children could benefit as well. This really helped improve my daughter's attention and behaviors. I really

feel this program was the best dynamic intervention that had been offered at the school."

Parent:
"My son made great improvement overall in his behaviors at school. I feel his behaviors improved throughout the entire neurofeedback process, and I received fewer complaints from school personnel about his behaviors."

Parent:
"I had a lot of concern about my daughter's ability to read and finish her work. She often would lie to get out of doing her work and often engaged in peer conflict. She really enjoyed the sessions because she loved to vent and problem-solve with us. I am very happy with the results, which kept my daughter from being referred for special education services. My daughter's attitude changed, which helped me be more willing to listen to her."

Elementary School Teacher:
"I have two students who have been participating in the program. I have seen an increase in focus and attention in both students—one more than the other. He has shown an increase in attention, working memory, and executive functioning skills. He is more willing to participate. The other student who is resistant to the task has continued to struggle with impulsiveness and focus. I believe the program has great benefit."

Elementary School Administrator:
"We have seen significant progress with these students both behaviorally and academically. This is assessed by the amount of office visits and assessments. Two of the students involved have had no incidents for the first two weeks of school and showed improvement at the end of the last school year. As their behavior and focus improves, we will continue to monitor their academic progress. We are excited to be a part of this program."

Director of Special Education:
"I always found the neurofeedback program to be very interesting and knew it would be great to implement as an early intervention. I believe in neurofeedback, and the results of this program were very significant and helped our students. I believe it would be very helpful to have this program embedded in the school as an ongoing alternative intervention. It provides a great deal of useful information and is an effective way to gather information on how to support our students and specifically on how they learn."

Elementary School Principal:
"I found that the neurofeedback program was a good intervention to implement prior to making a referral to special education for our students who have difficulty with attention and behaviors. I am excited to do anything needed to get neurofeedback started at my school."

Elementary Teacher:
"As a teacher, I was so interested in the neurofeedback program that I would like to try it for myself. I found the process to be very interesting and helpful for my students."

School Occupational Therapist:
"After Dr. Britt, our school psychologist, completed her doctoral program, I requested a copy of her dissertation to better understand how neurofeedback can go hand-in-hand with Occupational Therapy services in the school. Before Dr. Britt's program, I never understood the auditory and visual aspects of how students learn. This was an eye-opening process for me that contained so much valuable information. I provide fine and gross motor training, but I did not understand how auditory and visual processing problems would affect how I need to interact with my students."

School Superintendent:
"This neurofeedback program does not replace existing programs; it adds to the intervention tools we are able to provide to our students.

The neurofeedback program is an innovative process that helps us better address the needs of today's students. This program has changed the perception of what behaviors mean in the classroom since we now understand how auditory and visual processing problems can interfere with learning. The neurofeedback program provided teachers with new intervention tools that were relevant for each child who was struggling in the classroom."

School Psychologist:
"This neurofeedback program helped us develop a bridge between general education and special education collaborations. The program allowed students to receive earlier interventions in a way that clarified specific areas of strengths and weaknesses. This valuable information helped the team create better interventions. It gave teachers the right tools to implement in the classroom and for other staff members, tools for nonstructured times with our students.

It was a well-rounded way to gather information on a student and succeeded in preventing some of our students from being referred to special education. We found that many of them were having difficulties with auditory and visual processing versus having an actual deficit.

The program also helped us develop better rapport between parents and school personnel. It helped school personnel understand how to better maintain consistent and accurate support for our students at home and at school. So the program helped build better collaboration between the school and the parents. And parents and teachers were seeing eye-to-eye on the child's needs, which led to parents trusting school personnel. This improved trust and opened opportunities for other interventions. For example, one of our parents had not been open to allowing counseling, but with the improved rapport, the parent was more willing to consider this option for their child.

From the level of school personnel to district personnel, it brought clarity on how to address gaps in the programing and support by bringing more specificity to the supports provided at the general education level. It also provided school psychologists with a different way to work with students in a one-on-one process instead of only providing testing services. I found it was more rewarding to have a continuous opportunity to help a student versus only interacting in a testing environment. This then opened the door for more collaboration with the student and the school psychologist. Our field is known to work more with the teachers, and this gave me an opportunity to work directly with the students."

Elementary Children Who Participated:
At the end of the pilot project, the school psychologist shared that many of the children who initially participated prior to the school closures requested to continue with the neurofeedback program. They told their teachers and the school psychologist that they missed being a part of the program.

School Board Members:
School board members were interested in the changes in negative behaviors in the classroom—that included students throwing chairs— and said they were enlightened to know how behaviors have morphed over the years. In addition, they expressed appreciation in learning about how behaviors are the language of a child—a way of communicating— and how a child overwhelmed with auditory and visual processing problems can impact the classroom.

The board members better understood the children's reactions and what they mean for students in today's classrooms. The members gained insight as to how this information supports the changes in behaviors based on how students learn. They had an increased awareness about why the school needs to provide an alternative method of communication for a student with a visual processing problem and questioned why the school would use a visual schedule with such children.

In addition, board members were better informed about current classroom challenges in teasing out how auditory and visual processing problems look in the classroom and how this can cause difficulty in reading, copying, and the ability to follow instructions. The neurofeedback program brought clarity to the board members regarding what teachers are facing in the classroom.

*   *   *

It's my deepest hope that more schools will see the value in implementing a neurofeedback program within school settings. There are so many benefits to doing so. By providing this as an embedded service, we're able to provide neurofeedback sessions more consistently. Teachers and parents are more aligned with regard to the strengths and weaknesses of each child, which helps both parents and teachers be more consistent in supporting them. In addition, school administrations see direct benefits from this innovative service through reduced referrals for behavioral interventions and a financial benefit from reduced and unnecessary referrals to special education.

By identifying specific auditory and visual processing weaknesses, then strengthening those weaknesses, children are more likely to remain in the general education classroom and require fewer academic supports to do so. As I have said for years, everyone wins!

CHAPTER 13

FINDING A LASTING SOLUTION

Throughout these pages, I have strived to convey that hope exists for children who have learning difficulties or emotional challenges that are getting in the way of their ability to do their best in life.

The stories of the children in this book represent the hope that exists for all children. As you have learned, they exhibit a wide variety of behaviors that are often misinterpreted. When parents learn there is an actual *cause* for their child's behaviors and, just as importantly, that there is a *solution*, their world changes.

Although I have shared just a few stories with you, I have witnessed hundreds of such children improving their auditory and visual processing abilities. I have watched them become more self-confident, happier, less stressed, and more capable of handling life's ups and downs.

To be fair, each child's results are as unique as their challenges. Some take longer to achieve results, some take less time, and not everyone will benefit to the same degree. The process and results depend on many factors. However, anyone has the ability to improve their brain functioning. In fact, we have worked with professional athletes who wanted to put a little more edge on their game. One young woman was getting ready to compete in a gymnastics event and wanted a "tune-up." When she returned, she walked in wearing five medals around her neck and beaming about her success.

Neurofeedback is a game-changer for those who are struggling to learn, who have been diagnosed with conditions such as ADHD, anxiety, learning disabilities, oppositional defiant disorder (ODD), intermittent explosive disorder (IED), panic, trauma, and even chronic pain. It works because it deals with the neuroplasticity (flexibility) of the brain. And the good news is that age isn't a factor, as the brain is resilient and capable of change.

Almost anyone can change their brain. In fact, a few years back, we reversed the early onset of dementia in a woman entering her 80s, as independently confirmed by her physician, who didn't know she was participating in neurofeedback. Likewise, I didn't know she was on the brink of the dementia diagnosis. She asked for help to improve her memory, which we found to be weak. She participated in 40 neurofeedback sessions, and when she returned to her physician, he asked her what she had been doing because she'd improved her cognitive functioning several points on his assessment. As a result, she was no longer on the brink of the dementia.

So brain changes are possible. No longer do we need to believe that life is a downhill slide after a certain age. All of us can benefit from a tune-up. We have worked with people from ages three to 91. Each came for different reasons, but all held the same hope—to improve their brain functioning for a better quality of life. Generally, most children need to be at least six years of age to follow instructions and participate, but some who are younger can benefit on a case-by-case assessment.

Seeking Help

If you or someone you know is struggling, please reach out for assistance. Auditory and visual processing problems can have a detrimental effect on both children and adults. As we have seen in the stories in this book, children with unaddressed processing problems can end up in a great deal of trouble, even to the point of becoming suicidal.

I wrote this book during the pandemic, and as we emerge from that challenging time, more and more teenagers and children are being diagnosed with emotional and psychological conditions. So much of this can be attributed to what I believe is a complex trauma response to the fear that has pervaded our world during these last couple of years.

Without going too far into the reasons why, suffice it to say that the brain is hardwired for fear. This hardwiring is good for keeping us alive in some instances, but it isn't good when the fight or flight survival mechanism is on constant or prolonged high alert. Extended fight or flight response patterns can lead to the development of post-traumatic stress disorder (PTSD). Long-term exposure to seemingly unsolvable problems can also result in PTSD or trauma-based response patterns, elevated anxiety, or an onset of depressive symptoms.

Neurofeedback is an effective intervention in treating trauma regardless of the cause, helping the brain remember (or relearn) how to relax, and then hardwiring in the calmness the person seeks. In fact, I have treated a number of veterans[1] and children with trauma over the past decade, with many finding relief for the first time in years. Being able to avoid talk therapy is one of the benefits of neurofeedback when treating trauma, as talk therapy has been known to aggravate PTSD symptoms for some traumatized individuals.

There are many types of neurofeedback available (see Appendix A for a description of artifact corrected neurofeedback that I use), and it's wise to check the credentials of the person or company providing the services. This is particularly important when considering apps or other types of do-it-yourself interventions. Although I have nothing against do-it-yourself approaches and believe they can be helpful, most of them fail to include a professional assessment to determine a person's true needs and generally offer a one-size-fits-all approach. As seen throughout this book, the observed symptoms and behaviors are often misinterpreted as some other type of condition. The wrong diagnosis simply won't lead to the right kind of intervention. Some benefits might be gained, but the results won't be the same as a clinically based, professionally guided intervention based on the unique needs of the person.

In closing, it's my hope that you find the solution to the challenges your child is experiencing. If I can be of assistance, please contact me through my website at www.conniemcreynolds.com or email me at connie@mcreyno.com. For more information about remote professional neurofeedback services offered through my clinic and other sources of support, please see page 149.

I wish you and your child all the best in life!

ACKNOWLEDGEMENTS

As I have lived the experience of writing my first book, it has been with the constant support of friends and family who have encouraged me and believed my work can make a difference in the world.

In particular, I want to thank my mother who passed more than a decade ago. She taught second grade for 32 years in the same classroom in a small rural town in the Midwest. It was she who set the stage for my work without me even knowing it at the time.

Thank you also to my beloved Aunt Billye who was my cheerleader, always believing in me, and with whom I shared a special connection.

My dear Aunt Golda, who at the time of this writing approaches her 100th birthday. She has been an inspiration of perseverance and courage.

My valued friends include my lifelong friend, Cindy, with whom I have traveled life's ups and downs.

Brian, whose lifelong friendship has spanned many decades.

Jim, who has been a constant stalwart.

Ron, who is always good for a late-night chat.

Sharyn and Diane, who encourage my continued expansion and growth.

Rob, who has been a constant work companion from the beginning of the first clinic and who was always able to open closed doors.

Peg, whose consistent interest in the book provided encouragement.

Mike and Rose, Michael M., Mike O., and Jaryl, whose friendships have been priceless for more than two decades.

Thank you all for believing in me and this book.

To the clinicians and technicians who have been so dedicated to the goal of helping children and adults improve their quality of life, thank you. For all the nights you stayed late, provided comic relief, and shared the joy of success as children grew into their potential to show the world they were capable and able to thrive. A special thank you to Val, who has been invaluable with her consistent support and dedication to our work over the years.

The elementary school pilot project was accomplished through the efforts of the school psychologist, Dr. Cynthia Britt, who gained the support of the school administration, the school board, and the teachers. Due to her interest in neurofeedback, she facilitated the elementary pilot project and completed her dissertation assessing the impact in a school setting. Thank you for jumping on board to make the pilot project a success in demonstrating that we can do more within a school setting to help children who are struggling and for providing descriptions of the 504 and IEP processes.

And finally, I want to say a special thank you to all the parents who trusted me enough to bring their children to my clinics. Each and every one of you helped solve the riddle of ADHD as I developed more insight into what was causing learning, attention, and behavioral problems in your children. Understanding the real cause of the symptoms of ADHD and finding a lasting solution has been a pinnacle of my clinical career. Your bravery in seeking an alternative way to help your children is the fuel that forged this book. Knowing there are millions of children in the world who could benefit from this knowledge keeps me focused on expanding the awareness of what we do. Thank you for sharing your personal struggles and fears as we found a solution for your children.

Remote Neurofeedback Services

Remote neurofeedback services provide access to the same services available in my clinics but you participate from home. You work with a clinician at a scheduled time and receive the same assessments and neurofeedback services as if you were attending in person.

A free 15-minute consultation can be scheduled to discuss the technology and licensing requirements for remote services. Some limitations may exist depending on internet speed and other factors.

Contact Dr. Connie McReynolds for more information.

Email: connie@mcreyno.com

Website: www.conniemcreynolds.com

Educational Consultation Services

Educational consultation services are available to obtain guidance on 504, IEP, and ISP service plans to support your child at school.

Even if your child does not qualify for a 504, IEP or ISP plan, it may be beneficial to identify the types of accommodations and learning supports that will enhance your child's ability to succeed in school.

Without a true understanding of the way auditory and visual processing problems affect your child's ability to learn, parents (and teachers) are often at a loss as to how to help children succeed at home and in school.

Contact Dr. Connie McReynolds to schedule a free 15-minute discovery call.

Email: connie@mcreyno.com

Website: www.conniemcreynolds.com

ARTIFACT CORRECTED NEUROFEEDBACK

To better understand what artifact corrected neurofeedback is, it is necessary to define the term artifact.[1] As used here, the term 'artifact' refers to facial movements that can affect EEG signals in a neurofeedback system. For neurofeedback processes, research has shown that different kinds of signals can be detected by the EEG unit that are different from brain waves. These different kinds of signals are called electromyographical (EMG) signals that come from the person's scalp, eyes, facial muscles, tongue, and even their heart.

EMG signals are referred to as artifacts and need to be corrected (removed).[2] Because EMG signals are one thousand times stronger than EEG signals, they can contaminate, mimic, and obscure EEG data.[3] As LaMarca reported, "EMG artifact has the potential to degrade, if not entirely negate, the neurofeedback training process.[4] Research has demonstrated that facial EMG activity can create very high-amplitude artifact signals that contaminate the EEG frequencies between 0.025 and 32 Hz5, which is the range of the most commonly trained neurofeedback frequency bands."

So the term artifact corrected means the neurofeedback system is able to remove the unwanted artifacts (EMG signals) from the EEG measurements. Research has demonstrated that in doing so, brain training results are improved. Specifically, LaMarca found that by using artifact corrected neurofeedback, participants in his double-blind research study saw significantly greater improvements in auditory and visual processing abilities than participants who used non-artifact corrected neurofeedback.[6]

DESCRIPTION OF IVA2 SCORES

IVA2 Global and Standard Composite Scores[1]

The IVA2 provides nine global composite scores to help understand the various ways ADHD-type problems can be identified by this assessment.

IVA2 Measure	Description of Measure
Full Scale Response Control Quotient (FRCQ)	Based on six primary visual and auditory scales each and equal weights (not an average) of ARCQ and VRCQ scales.
Auditory Response Control Quotient (ARCQ)	Derived from auditory Prudence, Consistency, and Stamina scales
Visual Response Control Quotient (VRCQ)	Derived from visual Prudence, Consistency, and Stamina scales
Full Scale Attention Quotient (FAQ)	Based on six primary visual and auditory scales each based on equal measures of visual and auditory Vigilance, Focus, and Speed

IVA2 Measure	Description of Measure
Auditory Attention Quotient (AAQ)	Based on equal measures of auditory Vigilance, Focus, and Speed
Visual Attention Quotient (VAQ)	Based on equal measures of visual Vigilance, Focus, and Speed
Sustained Full Scale Attention Quotient (SFAQ)	Combined global measure of the SAAQ and SVAQ global scales
Sustained Auditory Attention Quotient (SAAQ)	Provides a global measure of a person's ability to respond to auditory stimuli under low demand conditions
Sustained Visual Attention Quotient (SVAQ)	Provides a global measure of a person's ability to respond to visual stimuli under low demand conditions

APPENDIX C

IVA2 DEFINITIONS

IVA2 Assessment Rating Definitions[1]

The Attention scales for auditory and visual processing are Vigilance, Focus, and Speed:

- The **Vigilance** scale measures problems related to inattention. People with low Vigilance scores may appear to be negligent or indifference. In contrast, when individuals score high on Vigilance they are described as watchful, alert, and attentive.

- The **Focus** scale is sensitive to variability in responses and can indicate problems related to "drifting off." Low scores on the Focus scale suggest the person has trouble remaining attentive and may have difficulty tuning out distractions such as sounds or activity taking place around them. They may be viewed as erratic or inconsistent. In contrast, a high Focus score relates to the person who is directed, efficient, concentrated, steady, or conscientious. People with a high Focus score may be better able to "tune out" distractions.

- The **Speed** scale is related to mental processing or how quickly a person can respond to information. An individual with a low Speed score may be mentally slow or may tend to delay.

In contrast, when individuals score high on Speed scale their performance is described as quick, fast, rapid, and swift.

The Response Control scales for auditory and visual processing are Prudence, Consistency, and Stamina:

- **Prudence** is a measure of impulsivity, or of the ability to stop, think and not automatically react. A person with a low Prudence score can be described as having problems with impulse control. People with low Prudence scores may demonstrate tendencies toward carelessness, thoughtlessness, or over-reactivity. In contrast, individuals with a high score on Prudence are described as careful to consider circumstances and possible consequences, mindful, and cautious.

- **Consistency** is a measure of the ability to perform in a generally reliable manner over time. A low Consistency score suggests the person may have difficulties keeping his or her attention directed. Low Consistency scale scores may be due to wandering of attention causing the person to stray off-task more than others without this problem. In contrast, individuals with a high Consistency score are described as disciplined, purposeful, harmonious thinking, with efficient, coherent, reliable and dependable mental processing. These individuals can ignore or inhibit distracting thoughts, feelings or environmental stimuli.

- **Stamina** is a measure of the increase or decrease in a person's response time speed during the test. Stamina can be useful in identifying difficulty maintaining a sustained effort over time. When a person has a low Stamina score, they can be described as having limited attentional energy and difficulty maintaining their speed of mental processing.

The **Fine Motor Hyperactivity** Scale provides additional information by recording off-task behaviors with the mouse, including multiple clicks, spontaneous clicks during instruction periods, anticipatory clicks, and holding the mouse button down. In behavioral terms, the Fine Motor Hyperactivity score quantifies fidgetiness and restlessness associated with small motor hyperactivity.

APPENDIX D

DIFFERENCES BETWEEN IEPS, 504 PLANS, AND INDIVIDUAL SERVICE PLANS

Individualized Educational Plans (IEP) and 504 Plans are offered through a public school.

The **IEP** is part of the Individuals with Disabilities Education Act (IDEA). It is a written document developed for each public school child who is eligible for special education. It is designed to meet your child's unique educational needs guaranteeing the necessary supports and services that are agreed upon.

Section 504 is a part of the Rehabilitation Act of 1973 that prohibits discrimination based upon disability. It is an anti-discrimination civil rights statute that requires the needs of students with disabilities to be met as adequately as the needs of the non-disabled are met.

Individual Service Plan (ISP) is offered through a private school. Private schools are not required to offer special education services although some may do so. Some private schools offer ISPs for specialized services within their own system; however, most specialized services are provided through the Local Education Agency (LEA) versus the school. Due to limited funding, these services may be similar, but fewer than those provided through a public school.

Description	IEP	504	Individual Service Plan
What It Does	An IEP spells out the services, supports, and specialized instruction your child with a disability will receive in school. These services are provided at no cost to parents.	Provides services and changes to the learning environment to enable students to learn alongside their peers. As with an IEP, a 504 plan is provided at no cost to families.	A service plan spells out the special education and related services the LEA will make available to your child. These services are provided at no cost to parents. But your child may not be able to receive these services at the private school. Instead, the LEA can require your child to go to a public school for services like speech therapy sessions.
What Law Applies	The Individuals with Disabilities Education Act (IDEA). This is a federal special education law for children with disabilities.	Section 504 of the Rehabilitation Act of 1973. This is a federal civil rights law to stop discrimination against people with disabilities.	§34 CFR 300.130 through §300.144 of IDEA is a specific section that describes how services are provided to children in private school.

Description	IEP	504	Individual Service Plan
Who's Eligible	To qualify for an IEP, your child must: • Have one of the 13 disabilities covered under IDEA • Need special education for their disability in order to successfully benefit from and access a general education curriculum	To get a 504 plan, there are two requirements: 1. A child (age 3-22) has *any* disability. Section 504 covers a wide range of different struggles in school. 2. The disability must interfere with the child's ability to learn in a general education classroom. Section 504 has a broader definition of a disability than IDEA. 504 states that a disability must substantially limit one or more basic life activities. This can include learning, reading, communicating, and thinking. This is why a child who doesn't qualify for an IEP might still be able to get a 504 plan.	To qualify for a service plan, a child must: • Be placed in a private school by the parents, not as an out-of-district placement • Have one of the 13 disabilities covered under IDEA • Need special education in order to successfully benefit from and access a general education curriculum

Description	IEP	504	Individual Service Plan
Independent Educational Evaluation	Families can ask the school district to pay for an (IEE) by an outside expert. The district doesn't have to agree. Families can always pay for an outside evaluation themselves, but the district may not give it much weight.	Does not allow families to ask for an IEE. As with an IEP evaluation, families can always pay for an outside evaluation themselves.	Families can always pay for an outside evaluation themselves, but the school may not give it much weight.
Who Creates the Plan	An IEP must be created by a team that includes: • A parent or legal guardian • A general education teacher • A special education teacher • A professional who can interpret evaluation results • A school administrator who knows about general and special education and who oversees special education services at the school	The rules about who is on the 504 team are less specific than for an IEP. A 504 plan is created by a team of people who are familiar with the child and who understand the evaluation data and special services options. This might include: The child's parent or caregiver General and special education teachers The school principal	A service plan must be created by the same people who make up an IEP team, as well as a representative of the private school.

Description	IEP	504	Individual Service Plan
What's In It	The IEP sets learning goals and describes the services the school will provide. It's a written document. The most important things the IEP must include: • The child's present levels of academic and functional performance—how the child is currently doing in school • Annual education goals for the child and how the school will track progress • The services the child will get—this may include special education, related, supplementary, and extended school year services • The timing of services—when they start, how often they occur, and how long they last • Any accommodations—changes to the child's learning environment	There is no standard 504 plan. Unlike an IEP, a 504 plan is not required to be a written document. A 504 plan generally includes the following: Specific accommodation supports, or services for the child Names of who will provide each service Name of the person responsible for ensuring the plan is implemented	A service plan does not have to ensure your child is provided with FAPE (free appropriate public education); however, services are to be equitable.

Description	IEP	504	Individual Service Plan
	• Any modifications—changes to what the child is expected to learn or know • How the child will participate in standardized tests • How the child will be included in general education classes and school activities		
Parent Consent	Parents must provide written consent for the school to evaluate your child. They also have to provide written consent before the school can provide the services in an IEP.	A parent or caregiver's consent is required for the school district to evaluate your child.	A parent must provide written consent for a child to be evaluated. The LEA will conduct the evaluation. A parent might request that the LEA in which the private school is located evaluate your child instead of the LEA in your local district. But the LEA will make the final decision.

Description	IEP	504	Individual Service Plan
Your Rights and Your Child's Rights	IDEA requires public schools to provide services to students in the least restrictive environment (LRE).

Parents have a say in the educational decisions for their children. Under IDEA, there are specific rights and protections for parents, as well as for children with learning and thinking differences.

These are called procedural safeguards. | There are fewer rights and safeguards in the 504 process.

Parents have a right to receive notice regarding the identification, evaluation, and/or placement of your child.

Examine relevant records pertaining to your child.

Request an impartial hearing with respect to the district's actions if there is a dispute about the 504 process. | Parents have a say in the educational decisions for your child. LEAs must evaluate students in private schools who may need special education.

If a parent thinks the LEA has failed to identify or evaluate their child, they can follow due process procedures.

Parents don't have due process rights if they are concerned a school isn't providing a FAPE. |
| How Often Reviewed and Revised | An IEP must be reviewed at least once a year.

Your child must also be re-evaluated every three years to see if services are still needed. | The rules vary by state. Generally, a 504 plan is reviewed each year and a reevaluation is done every three years or when needed. | IDEA says a service plan must be reviewed "to the extent appropriate" as often as an IEP.

It doesn't specify how often a service plan must be updated. |

See Reference Section for sources.

ANTONIO'S INITIAL ASSESSMENT IVA2 COMPREHENSIVE REPORT (ABRIDGED)

Name: Antonio

Age: 14 Sex: M

The IVA2 CPT (Integrated Visual & Auditory 2 Continuous Performance Test) is a test of attention and impulsivity that measures responses to intermixed auditory and visual stimuli. The quotient scores for all of the IVA2 scales are reported as standard scores (Mean = 100, SD = 15).

VALIDITY OF IVA2 TEST RESULTS

The main test results were found to be valid. All global and primary test scale scores can be interpreted without reservation. This individual's response pattern did not reveal any apparent abnormalities in his responses to either visual or auditory test stimuli. The examiner can proceed in an interpretation of all visual and auditory test scores without reservation.

SUMMARY OF TEST RESULTS FOR
THE IVA2 GLOBAL SCALES

The Full Scale Response Control Quotient is a global measure of the overall ability for this individual to regulate his responses and respond appropriately. This individual's overall global quotient scale score for the **Full Scale Response Control** scale was 105. This score fell in the average range. His **Auditory Response Control** quotient scale score was 111. This global scale score fell in the above average range. The **Visual Response Control** quotient scale score for this individual was 98. This global scale score fell in the average range.

The Full Scale Attention Quotient provides a measure of an individual's overall ability to accurately and quickly respond while maintaining focus. This individual's overall quotient score on the **Full Scale Attention** scale was 83. This global scale score fell in the mildly impaired range. His **Auditory Attention** quotient scale score was 87, and this global scale score fell in the slightly impaired range. The **Visual Attention** quotient scale score for this individual was 85. This global scale score was classified as falling in the slightly impaired range.

The Combined Sustained Attention quotient scale score provides a global measure of a person's ability to accurately and quickly respond in a reliable manner to stimuli under low demand conditions. In addition, it includes the ability to sustain attention and be flexible when things change under high demand conditions. These are reported as separate scale scores for both the auditory and visual modalities. This individual's global quotient score on the **Combined Sustained Attention** scale was 60. This score fell in the extremely impaired range. His global **Auditory Sustained Attention** quotient scale score was 74, and it fell in the moderately impaired range. The global **Visual Sustained Attention** quotient scale score for this individual was 61. This score was found to fall in the severely impaired range.

ATTENTION PRIMARY SCALES
Vigilance, Acuity, and Elasticity

Vigilance is a Primary scale that measures general attentional ability. This person's **Auditory Vigilance** quotient scale score was 87, which falls in the slightly impaired range. This individual showed a few problems with his general auditory attentional functioning that may on occasion affect his ability to perform adequately and to process auditory information accurately. He missed a few key auditory stimuli. Thus, he is likely to have a few problems with listening and processing auditory information in the school environment. Environmental stressors and social distractors may exacerbate his auditory attention problems at times.

This individual's quotient score was 76 on the **Auditory Acuity** scale. This quotient score was in the mildly to moderately impaired range. The Auditory Acuity scale showed that his ability to pay attention under low demand conditions to the auditory targets was mildly to moderately impaired. In other words, he had significant problems remaining alert when the non-targets were prevalent. This dysfunction in auditory attention indicates that he is likely to "tune out" periodically when there is little demand to perform, unless he is actively engaged in the task at hand. Behavioral interventions need to be considered to keep him on task and better manage his problems sustaining attention. Cognitive behavioral exercises may be beneficial for him as a way to develop his ability to maintain attention to routine tasks or uninteresting school assignments.

This individual's **Auditory Elasticity** quotient scale score was 106. This quotient score fell in the average range. The Auditory Elasticity scale showed a strength in his ability to be mentally flexible and make accurate responses under high demand conditions. In other words, this individual was able to maintain his attention and remain alert, even after inhibiting his response to the non-target. However, under low demand conditions, he showed difficulties in auditory attentional functioning that were discussed above.

He was found to attend relatively better under high demand conditions with respect to his ability to respond accurately to auditory targets than under low demand conditions. He became relatively less attentive under low demand conditions and showed difficulty sustaining his auditory attention when the test task did not actively engage him, as shown by his relatively greater impairment in the Auditory Acuity quotient scale score. Consequently, this individual is most prone to have difficulty attending to auditory stimuli unless the environment or motivational factors require him to be actively engaged. Individuals with this type of problem may generally "tune out" more often under low demand conditions. Problems are likely to manifest in terms of incomplete work or failure to fully perform assigned tasks that are auditory in nature. Individuals who have this type of auditory attentional deficit may benefit from accommodations that help them to stay on task, such as external reminders or immediate feedback of off-task behaviors. In addition, computerized exercises to help them learn how to better sustain their auditory attention and multi-modal sensory instructional techniques are likely to increase their ability to stay engaged and attentive.

This person's **Visual Vigilance** quotient scale score of 84 fell in the mildly impaired range. His general visual attentional functioning showed some problems that will sometimes impact his ability in some areas of his life to perform successfully. He exhibited moments of inattention to key visual stimuli. This is likely to be reflected by occasional issues in the school environment involving difficulties in him being able to maintain visual attention. Social distractions and environmental stressors may worsen his deficits in visual attention. He may also have good and bad days with respect to his attentional abilities.

He had a mildly to moderately impaired **Visual Acuity** scale with a quotient score of 77. He had a mild to moderate impairment in his ability to pay attention to visual targets under low demand conditions. Unless actively engaged in the task at hand, he is likely to "tune out" when there is little demand to perform. Behavioral interventions may help keep him on task and make him more aware of "drifting off." Cognitive behavioral exercises may assist him in developing his ability to sustain his attention to routine tasks or school assignments that don't interest him.

This individual's **Visual Elasticity** quotient scale score was average with a score of 106. The Visual Elasticity scale showed a strength in his ability to be mentally flexible and make accurate responses to targets under high demand conditions. After inhibiting his response to the non-target stimuli, he was able to maintain his attention and remain alert. However, as discussed above, he showed difficulties in visual attentional functioning under low demand conditions.

A significant difference was found in his abilities under low demand and high demand conditions, specifically in relation to the Visual Vigilance scale. He was found to attend relatively better under high demand conditions with respect to his ability to respond accurately to visual targets than under low demand conditions as reflected in his higher Visual Elasticity quotient scale score. He showed a greater relative ability to shift sets and was able to maintain his visual attention when the pace to perform was high. He showed difficulty sustaining his visual attention when the test task did not actively engage him, as shown by his relatively greater impairment in the Visual Acuity quotient scale score. Consequently, this individual is most prone to have difficulty attending to visual stimuli when the environment or motivational factors do not require him to be actively engaged. Individuals with this type of problem may generally "tune out" more often under low demand conditions. He is likely to fail to fully perform assigned tasks that are visual in nature. External reminders or immediate feedback of off-task behaviors are likely to be of benefit to him. Computerized exercises to help him learn how to better sustain his visual attention and multi-modal sensory instructional techniques are likely to increase his ability to stay engaged and attentive.

This individual's impairments in Vigilance occurred for both the auditory and visual modalities. Low scores in both of these sensory modalities are likely to lead to a compounding of problems in functioning. He showed no specific strengths in any one sensory modality that would enable him to compensate for his attention problems. This individual is likely to make errors of attention that will probably impact his home or school environment. Appropriate interventions will need to be considered with respect to these problems. Accommodations recommended above for both the visual and auditory modalities need to be considered in order to help him.

Focus, Dependability, and Stability
The Focus scale reflects an individual's ability to sustain attention reliably and not "drift off" or "tune out." Impairments in Focus result from relatively frequent slow response times to test stimuli that occur sporadically. These delays in response may occur due to momentary lapses in attention, confusion caused by deficits in working memory, episodic mental fatigue or deficits in sustaining attention.

This individual's **Auditory Focus** quotient scale score of 67 fell in the severely impaired range. Frequent delays in his response times to auditory test stimuli were found. This is likely to significantly impact his ability to process information. These lapses in auditory attention may lead to problems involving recall that affect the performance of this individual in a school environment. Learning new tasks, particularly when the information is presented verbally, is likely to be very challenging for him, and it will be necessary to review the material to help this person "fill in any gaps" in his learning experience. It may become evident that this individual "tunes out" when given verbal instructions. Accommodations may need to be made to help him stay alert in the school environment. This individual also needs to be encouraged to check the notes he takes during lectures or meetings, as "gaps" in his accuracy are likely to occur. Problems with emotional functioning may lead to learned helplessness, and assigned activities may be incorrectly done due to an incomplete comprehension of the verbal instructions given. Auditory cognitive behavioral exercises can help this person recognize in a supportive way when he momentarily loses his attention when listening. These exercises can also help this individual develop his ability to better sustain attention and to inhibit internal distractions and negative thoughts that may preoccupy him.

He showed some problems with respect to the **Auditory Dependability** scale. His quotient score on this scale was 83, which falls in the mildly impaired range. However, his problems with remaining focused were found to be less prevalent when the required pace to pay attention was slower. Thus, this individual may be better able to make efforts and learn in the school and work environments, if the pace of instruction or presentation of new auditory information is provided more slowly. He may need some modification of his environment in order to help him stay more actively engaged in auditory tasks. External reinforcement could also prove useful and will need to be considered as a way to stimulate him to be more resolute in sustaining his attention and perform more quickly. He may, though, at times be challenged by more routine tasks or tasks that are not intrinsically motivating for him. In these cases, the above modifications will need to be considered to help him.

A relative strength was found for him with respect to the **Auditory Stability** scale. His quotient score on this scale was 95, which falls in the average range. Consequently, he demonstrated the ability to make reliable responses to auditory stimuli under high demand conditions.

This person's **Visual Focus** quotient scale score of 91 fell in the average range. No problems were found for him with visual focus. During the IVA2 test, his response times were not excessively variable. He demonstrated that he could cope well with both internal and external visual distractions and stay focused visually.

His **Visual Dependability** scale showed some problems with remaining focused when the required pace to pay attention was less demanding. His quotient score on this scale was 88. Thus, this individual showed difficulty that may impact his efforts to learn and perform in the school environments. He may need some modification of his environment in order to help him stay more actively engaged in visual tasks. External reinforcements such as rewards or consistent prompting may prove useful as a way to stimulate him to improve his performance. Under stress or extremely demanding conditions, he may become challenged and have difficulty with routine tasks or tasks that are not intrinsically motivating for him. In these cases, the above modifications could very likely help him.

In respect to recognition reaction time, he was able to respond in a reliable manner as evidenced by the **Visual Stability** scale. His quotient score on this scale was 93, which falls in the average range. He demonstrated the ability to maintain his speed of response to visual stimuli under high demand conditions.

Speed, Quickness, and Swiftness
This individual's ability to process information and make decisions, as measured by the Speed scale, is an important variable that is likely to impact his performance in school settings with respect to being able to get work done within a reasonable time frame and with an acceptable degree of accuracy.

This individual's **Auditory Speed** quotient scale score of 119 falls in the above average range. This individual showed a strength in his overall auditory processing speed. His recognition reaction time falls within the above average range. His processing speed shows that he is above average with respect to his ability to perceive and respond to auditory stimuli. If problems exist with respect to listening skills, organizational abilities, working memory, emotional self-regulation, reading, or the ability to finish work tasks in a timely manner, the impact of environmental stimuli and social distractions needs to be evaluated and considered.

This individual's **Auditory Quickness** quotient scale score of 122 falls in the superior range. His quotient score on the **Auditory**

Swiftness scale was 95. This quotient score is interpreted as average. This individual's Auditory Quickness score is significantly higher than his Auditory Swiftness score. This indicates that he performed faster under high demand conditions (i.e., when the targets were frequent) as compared to low demand conditions (when the targets were rare). He was slower to a noticeable degree in his auditory processing speed under low demand conditions. He is likely to perform better in learning situations when the demand to perform is high and the tasks that he is required to do are engaging.

He had an average **Visual Speed** quotient scale score of 97. No problems were found with his overall visual processing speed. His recognition reaction time falls within the average range. His processing speed shows that he is able to perceive quickly and respond adequately to visual stimuli. If problems exist with respect to organizational abilities, visual memory, emotional self-regulation, or the ability to finish work tasks in a timely manner, the impact of other causal factors will need to be evaluated and considered. These factors may include environmental stimuli, social distractions, and emotional, cognitive, or psychological problems.

This individual's **Visual Quickness** quotient scale score of 99 falls in the average range. He had a mildly impaired **Visual Swiftness** scale score of 80. For visual targets, he was significantly faster under high demand conditions, as reflected by his higher Visual Quickness score in comparison to Visual Swiftness. He was slower to a noticeable degree in his visual processing speed under low demand conditions when the targets were rare. Consequently, he is likely to perform better in learning situations when there is a high expectation for performance and when he is actively engaged in the task.

RESPONSE CONTROL PRIMARY SCALES
Prudence and Reliability
Prudence is a measure of impulsivity as defined by errors of commission.

This individual's **Auditory Prudence** quotient scale score of 107 fell in the average range. This individual was found to be functioning in the average range with respect to his ability to inhibit responses to non-target auditory stimuli. Thus, he is able to control his responses and not be excessively distracted by auditory stimuli in his environment. He can shift sets well.

He exhibited some problems with respect to the **Auditory Reliability** scale. His quotient score on this scale was 80, which falls in the mildly impaired range. This pattern of responding indicates periods of random, idiopathic, impulsive clicks to non-target auditory stimuli, in other words, clicking to the non-targets under low demand conditions. The impact of this deficit will in most cases be mild, manifesting as careless errors or inappropriate responses to auditory stimuli in the home and school environments. Given his relatively poor score for the Reliability scale as compared to the Auditory Prudence scale, he may perform better on tasks that are more engaging and demanding. His pattern of responding indicates that he is likely at times to become bored and in these cases his mind may wander; leading to unusual, off-task responses.

This person's **Visual Prudence** quotient scale score of 94 fell in the average range. No problems with inhibition to non-target visual stimuli were identified. This individual demonstrated an average ability to control his responses and inhibit appropriately to non-target visual stimuli. This score on the Prudence scale indicates that he is unlikely to be distracted by visual stimuli. He showed the ability to regulate and shift sets on the IVA2 test which demonstrated self-control for visual stimuli when the environment frequently changes.

No problems were found for his **Visual Reliability** scale. The quotient score on this scale was 105, which falls in the average range. He was able to avoid making impulsive idiopathic errors that would lead to careless or inappropriate responses in his home and school environments.

Consistency

The Consistency scale is a general measure of an individual's ability to respond reliably based on his reaction time.

This individual was severely impaired in his ability to be consistent in his responses to auditory stimuli. His **Auditory Consistency** quotient scale score was 67. This variability reflects a delay in his optimum response time that is likely to significantly impact his ability to process auditory information. Problems in memory due to erratic information processing may be prevalent. This individual may have difficulties learning new tasks in the school environment. Repetition of instructions or information presented to him may help him to better understand new material. It may be necessary to provide a more restrictive environment with less distractions to enable this individual to be more consistent in his mental processing. A slower pace in the presentation of new concepts may also facilitate his ability to master new ideas. This individual needs to be encouraged and reinforced to review and check his work as he is likely to be prone to make careless errors. Cognitive behavioral exercises designed to improve auditory processing and sustained attention need to be considered in order to enhance his ability to process instructional material and to help improve his memory functioning.

This individual's ability to be consistent in his responses to visual stimuli was mildly impaired. The **Visual Consistency** quotient scale score for this individual was 83. In order to sustain attention to visual stimuli when required, this individual will need to learn to ignore internal and external distractions. Cognitive training exercises are likely to help him to enhance his ability for sustained detailed visual attention and visual memory. Written materials should be made available so that he can review them and better comprehend any new concepts or ideas presented. Otherwise, gaps in learning may occur. Careless visual errors are also likely to impair the accuracy of his responses. He needs to be encouraged to review all written responses and to learn how to "catch his own errors."

Stamina

The Stamina scale is a measure of the individual's ability to sustain his speed of response time during the course of the test.

This individual's **Auditory Stamina** quotient scale score of 148 fell in the exceptional range. This person's response time to auditory stimuli became faster over the course of the test. He was able to increase his mental processing speed in the auditory domain during the test. In a school setting, he is likely to be capable of meeting the demand to perform and to achieve goals in a timely manner. In respect to his auditory processing speed, his work habits are likely to reflect the ability to increase his efforts and to "rise to the occasion" even when he is faced with challenging tasks.

He had an above average **Visual Stamina** quotient scale score of 119. He was able to increase his mental processing speed in the visual domain during the test. He is unlikely to have any significant deficits in terms of meeting the demand to perform and to achieve goals in a timely manner. In his work habits, he is likely to double his efforts and meet the demand even when he is faced with visually challenging work.

Strengths were found in this individual for both the auditory and visual domains of the Stamina scale. This individual is likely to be able to get his work done quickly because of his strengths in stamina. He showed the ability to process and maintain his attention to both visual and auditory information over time.

Fine Motor Hyperactivity

The Fine Motor Hyperactivity Quotient measures off-task, spurious, impulsive, and inappropriate fine motor activity using the mouse input device. A person who is squirmy, restless, or who doodles or fiddles with small objects may score low on this scale. These kinds of response tendencies may be described as fidgetiness and restlessness. Quotient scores above the average range are considered reflective of better controlled and more self-regulated responses.

This person's **Fine Motor Hyperactivity** quotient scale score was 111. His score fell in the above average range. He made no spontaneous responses while the instructions preceding the Warm-up and Practice sessions were being delivered. This above average quotient score for the Fine Motor Hyperactivity scale indicates no significant problems in fine motor hyperactivity.

The lack of problems shown on the Fine Motor Hyperactivity scale suggests that he is likely to be able to follow simple general rules and not demonstrate fidgetiness. In many cases, this above average score on the Fine Motor Hyperactivity scale is considered a positive indicator regarding his ability to refrain from distracting others while they are working. His above average quotient score is interpreted as reflecting a high degree of fine motor control that is likely to benefit this individual. He is very likely to be able to engage in controlled and directed responses with respect to his general motoric skills.

SYMPTOMATIC SCALES
Comprehension, Steadiness, and Reliability

The Comprehension scale is a measure of idiopathic errors both of commission and omission occurring under both low and high demand conditions.

This individual's **Auditory Comprehension** quotient scale score of 86 fell in the slightly impaired range. Generally, he exhibited only slight problems with functioning adequately in terms of the Auditory Comprehension scale. His response pattern indicates that he is not very likely to have difficulties related to comprehension unless he is stressed or significantly fatigued. Further discussion regarding any relative weaknesses or strengths is presented below for the Steadiness and Reliability scales that comprise the Comprehension scale.

His **Auditory Steadiness** quotient scale score was 92. This quotient score fell in the average range. No significant problems with attention to auditory stimuli for this individual as measured by the Steadiness scale were identified as occurring under high demand conditions.

This individual demonstrated that he understood the test rules when required to respond to auditory targets when they were prevalent. His scale score showed no impairment.

On the **Auditory Reliability** scale, he had a quotient score of 80. This quotient score fell in the mildly impaired range. He showed some problems with respect to the Auditory Reliability scale. His pattern of responding indicates that there were a few periods when he engaged in random or impulsive clicking to non-target auditory stimuli. The impact of his deficit is likely to be mild, manifesting as occasional careless errors or inappropriate responses to auditory stimuli in his home and/or school environment.

This individual's **Visual Comprehension** quotient scale score of 54 fell in the extremely impaired range. Severe problems were identified for this individual with respect to the **Visual Comprehension scale**. He made a large number of idiopathic errors, showing significant trouble with test performance and difficulties in following the test rules.

His **Visual Steadiness** quotient scale score was 16. This quotient score fell in the extremely impaired range. When the requirement to perform is high his ability to respond appropriately to visual stimuli was found to be significantly impaired. His pattern of responding suggested a number of possible factors that could account for his poor visual functioning, including gross negligence, an attitude of indifference, or visual working memory deficits. In any case, his scale scores on both the Visual Comprehension and Steadiness scales reveal major impairments involving visual attentional functioning.

He had a quotient score of 105 on the **Visual Reliability** scale. This quotient score was in the average range. No problems with respect to the Visual Reliability scale were identified for him. He made few impulsive idiopathic visual errors of commission. He responded well to visual stimuli under low demand test conditions and was careful not to make errors.

Persistence

This individual's **Auditory Persistence** quotient scale score of 90 fell in the average range. There was no significant difference in his auditory reaction time during the Cool-down as compared to the Warm-up. Thus, his quotient score on the Persistence scale did not indicate any problems with his motivation that would impair his functioning on the IVA2 test. Given that his Auditory Stamina quotient score fell in the exceptional range, he was not identified by the test as being mentally fatigued in his ability to respond to auditory stimuli. This pattern of responding suggests that he does not get fatigued easily when required to process auditory stimuli.

This person's **Visual Persistence** quotient scale score of 90 fell in the average range. No significant difference was found in his visual reaction time during the Cool-down as compared to the Warm-up. Thus, his quotient score on the Persistence scale did not indicate any problems with his motivation that would impact his functioning on the IVA2 test. Given that his Visual Stamina quotient score fell in the above average range, he was not found to show any mental or motoric fatigue in respect to his ability to respond to visual stimuli. This pattern of responding indicates that he is not likely to become easily fatigued when he has to process visual stimuli.

Sensory/Motor

This individual's **Auditory Sensory/Motor** quotient scale score of 122 fell in the superior range. This scale score was computed based on the mean of the three fastest reaction times of his auditory responses during the Warm-up test period. His auditory simple reaction time was faster than most peers his age. This superior score on the Sensory/Motor scale indicates that he is likely to be able to process and respond quickly to auditory stimuli. His quotient score on the Sensory/Motor scale did not reveal any problems with functioning that would impair his test performance or affect him in his life. Given that his Auditory

Speed quotient score fell in the above average range, he was not found to have difficulties related to his auditory recognition reaction time.

This person's **Visual Sensory/Motor** quotient scale score of 113 was in the above average range. The mean of his three fastest visual reaction times during the Warm-up test period was used in determining this scale score. His visual simple reaction time scores were higher than most individuals his age. This above average score on the Sensory/Motor scale indicates that he is generally able to quickly process and respond quickly to simple visual stimuli. His quotient score on the Sensory/Motor scale did not identify any problems with functioning that would impair his test performance or affect him in his daily life. Given that his Visual Speed quotient score fell in the average range, he was not found to have problems related to his Visual Speed reaction time.

IVA2 DIAGNOSTIC CONSIDERATIONS

Even though this individual's global Full Scale Response Control quotient scale score did not indicate a significant impairment in functioning, his global Sustained Visual Attention quotient scale score did reveal a severe impairment. In addition, a moderate impairment was found in respect to this individual's Sustained Auditory Attention quotient scale score. There were two Attention Primary scales that fell in the substantially impaired range. One scale (Auditory Reliability) measuring commission errors showed that he had significant response control deficits.

ANDREA'S SECOND ASSESSMENT IVA2 COMPREHENSIVE REPORT (ABRIDGED)

Name: Andrea

Age: 7 Sex: F

The IVA2 CPT (Integrated Visual & Auditory 2 Continuous Performance Test) is a test of attention and impulsivity that measures responses to intermixed auditory and visual stimuli. The quotient scores for all of the IVA2 scales are reported as standard scores (Mean = 100, SD = 15).

VALIDITY OF IVA2 TEST RESULTS

The main test results were found to be valid. All global and primary test scale scores can be interpreted without reservation. This individual's response pattern did not reveal any apparent abnormalities in her responses to either visual or auditory test stimuli. The examiner can proceed in an interpretation of all visual and auditory test scores without reservation.

SUMMARY OF TEST RESULTS FOR
THE IVA2 GLOBAL SCALES

The Full Scale Response Control Quotient is a global measure of the overall ability for this individual to regulate her responses and respond appropriately. Factors that load on this scale include the ability to inhibit responses to non-targets, the consistency of recognition reaction times and the person's ability to maintain her mental processing speed during the IVA2 test. This individual's overall global quotient scale score for the **Full Scale Response Control** scale was 92. This score fell in the average range. Her **Auditory Response Control** quotient scale score was 95. This global scale score fell in the average range. The **Visual Response Control** quotient scale score for this individual was 92. This global scale score fell in the average range.

The Full Scale Attention Quotient provides a measure of an individual's overall ability to accurately and quickly respond while maintaining focus. This global scale primarily measures performance under low demand conditions. This individual's overall quotient score on the **Full Scale Attention** scale was 71. This global scale score fell in the moderately to severely impaired range. Her **Auditory Attention** quotient scale score was 80, and this global scale score fell in the mildly impaired range. The **Visual Attention** quotient scale score for this individual was 68. This global scale score was classified as falling in the moderately to severely impaired range.

The Combined Sustained Attention quotient scale score provides a global measure of a person's ability to accurately and quickly respond in a reliable manner to stimuli under low demand conditions. In addition, it includes the ability to sustain attention and be flexible when things change under high demand conditions. These are reported as separate scale scores for both the auditory and visual modalities. This individual's global quotient score on the **Combined Sustained Attention** scale was 57. This score fell in the extremely impaired range. Her global **Auditory Sustained Attention** quotient scale score was 60, and it fell in the extremely impaired range. The global **Visual**

Sustained Attention quotient scale score for this individual was 63. This score was found to fall in the severely impaired range.

The identified strengths, weaknesses, and interrelationships of the Auditory and Visual Response Control and Attention scales are reported and discussed below. The specific scales that comprise the Auditory and Visual Sustained Attention scales and their meanings are discussed in the sections related to the Primary Response Control and Attention scales. Also, a discussion is included in the sections below for the three Symptomatic scales: Comprehension, Persistence, and Sensory/Motor.

ATTENTION PRIMARY SCALES

Vigilance, Acuity, and Elasticity

Vigilance is a Primary scale that measures general attentional ability. This person's **Auditory Vigilance** quotient scale score was 71, which falls in the moderately to severely impaired range. This individual showed significant problems with her general auditory attentional functioning. These problems are likely to have a major impact on her ability to perform successfully in many areas of her life. During periods of the test, she failed to stay attentive to key auditory stimuli and was not able to sustain her auditory attention. Consequently, she is likely to have problems in the school environment in maintaining her auditory attention unless she is actively engaged or environmental demands to perform are clearly evident to her and enforced. Social distractors or stress may further exacerbate her attentional problems. She is likely to have "good and bad days" with respect to auditory attentional functioning.

This individual's quotient score was 86 on the **Auditory Acuity** scale. This quotient score was in the slightly impaired range. The Auditory Acuity scale showed that her ability to pay attention under low demand conditions to the auditory targets was slightly impaired. Some problems were found for her in being able to pay attention when the non-targets were prevalent. This finding suggests that she is likely to occasionally "tune out" and may do so when stressed or when performance is not inherently engaging. Social distractors may impact her attentional functioning and influence her ability to stay on task. Environmental changes may prove beneficial in correcting her auditory attentional functioning. Cognitive training may prove beneficial in improving her ability to perform routine tasks.

This individual's **Auditory Elasticity** quotient scale score was 65. This quotient score fell in the severely impaired range. Her lapses in attention specifically occurred immediately after being required to inhibit responding. This reflects difficulties in auditory attentional functioning and indicates that she had problems being able to quickly get "back on track." Cognitive training focusing on improving the speed of mental processing and mental flexibility may prove beneficial for her in correcting this "shift-set" deficit in auditory attentional functioning. An individual with these specific types of problems is likely to be very easily distracted and have problems with mental alertness as well. Compensatory techniques to increase her awareness of her problems in maintaining and accurately responding to changes in her environment need to be considered. In addition, cognitive training exercises to enhance attentional focus and response accuracy when the demand to perform is high are likely to benefit her.

This individual's ability to attend under high demand conditions significantly differed from her ability to respond accurately to auditory targets under low demand conditions. When the pace is slower, she showed the ability to attend relatively better and her response accuracy was higher. Individuals with this pattern are likely to benefit from accommodations that minimize auditory distractions in their environment and will generally do better if provided additional time to get work done, so that they do not feel pressured to perform.

This person's **Visual Vigilance** quotient scale score of 84 fell in the mildly impaired range. Her general visual attentional functioning showed some problems that will sometimes impact her ability in some areas of her life to perform successfully. She exhibited moments of inattention to key visual stimuli. This is likely to be reflected by occasional issues in the school environment involving difficulties in her being able to maintain visual attention. Social distractions and environmental stressors may worsen her deficits in visual attention. She may also have good and bad days with respect to her attentional abilities.

She had an average **Visual Acuity** scale with a quotient score of 90. In terms of visual attention, a relative strength was found in her ability to pay attention under low demand conditions, as shown in the Visual Acuity scale. This individual was able to maintain her attention and stay alert when the demand to perform was relatively low. However, her Elasticity scale showed significant problems in visual attentional functioning under high demand conditions that will need to be addressed.

This individual's **Visual Elasticity** quotient scale score was mildly to moderately impaired with a score of 78. Her lapses in attention showed difficulty in her visual attentional functioning which impaired her ability to quickly get "back on track." Cognitive training that focuses on improving her speed of mental processing may be helpful for her. She is likely to be very easily distracted and report difficulty with mental alertness. Compensatory techniques need to be considered to increase her awareness of her problems with accurately responding to changes in her environment.

A significant difference was found in her abilities under low demand and high demand conditions, specifically in regards to the Visual Vigilance scale. She is likely to have problems with respect to her visual attentional functioning more often when she has to shift sets or under conditions that distract her. Minimizing visual distractions in her environment is likely to improve performance. Providing accommodations with regards to additional time to get work done is likely to minimize stress on her and also would likely increase performance.

This individual's impairments in Vigilance occurred for both the auditory and visual modalities. Low scores in both of these sensory modalities are likely to lead to a compounding of problems in functioning. She showed no specific strengths in any one sensory modality that would enable her to compensate for her attention problems. This individual is likely to make errors of attention that will probably impact her home or school environment. Appropriate interventions will need to be considered with respect to these problems. Accommodations recommended above for both the visual and auditory modalities need to be considered in order to help her.

Focus, Dependability, and Stability
The Focus scale reflects an individual's ability to sustain attention reliably and not "drift off" or "tune out."

This individual's **Auditory Focus** quotient scale score of 102 fell in the average range. No significant problems with auditory focus were identified for her. She was able to maintain her auditory focus throughout the test.

On the IVA2 test, she showed the ability to respond reliably to auditory stimuli as evidenced by the **Auditory Dependability** scale. Her quotient score on this scale was 97, which falls in the average range. Her response times to auditory stimuli did not excessively vary under low demand conditions.

She was identified to show some problems in her ability to respond reliably as evidenced by the **Auditory Stability** scale. Her quotient score on this scale was 89, which falls in the slightly impaired range. Generally, she was able to maintain her processing speed under high demand conditions when the targets were prevalent. This pattern of responding indicates that she may at times be somewhat erratic in her responses to auditory stimuli and that she may, at times, be prone to make some errors when the demand for her to perform is high. Systematic cognitive training needs to be considered in order to help her improve the stability of her auditory attentional functioning.

This person's **Visual Focus** quotient scale score of 87 fell in the slightly impaired range. Most of the time this individual is able to process and stay focused on visual stimuli. Infrequent lapses in visual response times were found. These lapses in visual processing may be due to slight fatigue or to a preoccupation with distracting thoughts. She needs to be encouraged to ask for any information she misses due to her slight problems with visual focus, and she should learn to ask others for help when necessary. Generally, her problems with visual focus will only manifest in highly distracting environments or when she is emotionally upset. Cognitive training exercises can help her learn to be better focused to visual stimuli and to recognize how to maintain her visual attention.

She showed significantly greater problems in her variability of responding under low demand conditions as evidenced by the extremely impaired **Visual Dependability** scale of 53. This individual's problems with maintaining her speed of responding to visual stimuli were clearly evident when little demand was placed on her to maintain her sustained attention. She becomes more variable in her attentional functioning when she is not actively engaged in a task. Either environmental conditions will need to be modified or external reinforcements may need to be implemented to help her stay on task.

Significant problems were found for her with respect to the **Visual Stability** scale. Her quotient scale was moderately to severely impaired with a score of 69. This indicated she had problems with maintaining her processing speed reliably under high demand conditions when the targets were prevalent. She showed more variability in her responses when the pace of test was faster. This pattern of responding indicates that she is likely to be more erratic in her response time to visual stimuli and make more errors when the demand for her to perform is high. Systematic cognitive training to improve her processing speed and reliability in responding is likely to be the best approach to help her.

Speed, Quickness, and Swiftness

This individual's ability to process information and make decisions, as measured by the Speed scale, is an important variable that is likely to impact her performance in school settings with respect to being able to get work done within a reasonable time frame and with an acceptable degree of accuracy.

This individual's **Auditory Speed** quotient scale score of 86 falls in the slightly impaired range. This individual was slightly impaired in her auditory processing speed during the test. This problem is likely to have some impact on her ability to perform in different areas of her life. This deficit reflects slightly impaired mental processing speed to auditory stimuli. She is likely at times to have a little difficulty in listening, comprehending, and recalling verbal information presented to her. The impact of this slight deficit is likely to be minimal in her social interactions with others and in her ability to meet the demands of the school environment. Her problems in listening and processing auditory information are likely to occur only when she is stressed by very complex and challenging tasks. Occasionally, she may show some slight difficulties with working memory, but she would generally be expected to perform most auditory tasks at an adequate pace. Cognitive training exercises may help this individual to "normalize" her auditory processing speed. This individual may want to consider using various organizational techniques and tools in order to improve her functioning.

This individual's **Auditory Quickness** quotient scale score of 84 falls in the mildly impaired range. Her quotient score on the **Auditory Swiftness** scale was 92. This quotient score is interpreted as average. When the required pace to process auditory test stimuli was slower, she was able to respond quicker than when the demand to perform was high. This individual is not likely to respond well when pressured to perform. She is likely to do better when auditory information is presented to her more slowly.

She had a severely impaired **Visual Speed** quotient scale score of 67. This indicated she had a significant delay in her visual processing speed during the test. This deficit would be expected to have a major impact on her ability to perform in different areas of her life. This deficit reflects a very slow visual mental processing speed, and she is likely to be severely impaired in her ability to read and understand written instructions or directions. She will probably have difficulty with comprehension and recall of information presented to her in a visual format. She may also have some difficulty taking accurate and detailed notes in the classroom setting or in meetings, because these tasks require her to shift sets. She may be described as a "slow learner" in a school setting.

Her deficit in processing visual information quickly is likely to negatively impact her self-confidence. She may be easily discouraged and attempt to avoid tasks that she believes will be difficult. In some cases, her problem may manifest in the expression of her feelings of frustration or anger. She may also become irritable or lash out with negative verbal outbursts. Any of these types of emotional problems, if they occur, are likely to impair her social interactions with peers such that others avoid her, and, thus, further contributing to her negative self-image.

It is highly likely that her working memory is impacted by her mental processing speed, which in turn may significantly affect reading comprehension, visual recall, and her ability to complete multi-step tasks. She may also have poor organizational skills due to problems with setting priorities, staying on task, and following work through to completion. In some cases, she may avoid doing her required work altogether.

Cognitive training exercises which focus on improving visual processing speed and working memory are likely to be of benefit to her. A successful program could help her to become better organized in her thinking, and increase her ability to be an "active thinker." She is also likely to respond well to behavioral interventions that help her set priorities, stay on task, and "get the job done." Improvement in visual processing speed can help enable her to process visual information more accurately in the school environment. Due to her severe deficits in visual processing speed, additional compensatory strategies may also need to be explored in more detail.

This individual's **Visual Quickness** quotient scale score of 65 falls in the severely impaired range. She had a moderately impaired **Visual Swiftness** scale score of 72. No significant difference was found between the quotient scores for the Visual Quickness and Visual Swiftness scales. Her mean visual reaction time was generally the same under both high and low demand conditions.

This individual's significant impairments in Speed were evident for the visual modality. She was found to have some impairment for the auditory modality. Thus, she may benefit from interventions to help improve both her visual and auditory processing speed.

RESPONSE CONTROL PRIMARY SCALES

Prudence and Reliability

Prudence is a measure of impulsivity as defined by errors of commission. This individual's **Auditory Prudence** quotient scale score of 108 fell in the average range. This individual was found to be functioning in the average range with respect to her ability to inhibit responses to non-target auditory stimuli. Thus, she is able to control her responses and not be excessively distracted by auditory stimuli in her environment.

She did not demonstrate any problems with respect to the **Auditory Reliability** scale. Her quotient score on this scale was 95, which falls in the average range. Thus, she was able to avoid making impulsive idiopathic errors that would lead to careless or inappropriate responses in her home and school environments. This individual is likely to be able to be accurate in detailed tasks and to remember and follow rules well.

This person's **Visual Prudence** quotient scale score of 105 fell in the average range. No problems with inhibition to non-target visual stimuli were identified. This individual demonstrated an average ability to control her responses and inhibit appropriately to non-target visual stimuli. This score on the Prudence scale indicates that she is unlikely to be distracted by visual stimuli.

No problems were found for her **Visual Reliability** scale. The quotient score on this scale was 108, which falls in the average range. She was able to avoid making impulsive idiopathic errors that would lead to careless or inappropriate responses in her home and school environments. This individual is likely to be able to be accurate in detailed tasks and to remember and follow rules well.

Consistency

The Consistency scale is a general measure of an individual's ability to respond reliably based on her reaction time.

This individual was mildly impaired in her ability to be consistent in her responses to auditory stimuli. Her **Auditory Consistency** quotient scale score was 83. This individual will need to learn to ignore internal or external auditory distractions in order to improve her performance when sustained attention is required. Cognitive training exercises may help improve her ability to listen, attend, and follow multi-step directions. Training in auditory processing is likely to improve memory and functioning in a variety of other tasks as well. Written or taped presentation materials need to be provided to this individual so that she can review the concepts and ideas presented in order to "fill in the gaps." Reinforcement of "double-checking" her work is also recommended in order to minimize careless errors.

This individual's ability to be consistent in her responses to visual stimuli was moderately to severely impaired. The **Visual Consistency** quotient scale score for this individual was 69. Her impairment, as demonstrated by this very low quotient score on the Visual Consistency scale, is likely to significantly impact her functioning in her life. This deficit may be due to internal or external distractions. Consequently, the minimization of visual distractions in the environment could help her to respond more consistently and to reduce careless errors. Any visual instructional material should be available for her review in order to compensate for possible deficits in her ability to process new information quickly and reliably. She needs to be encouraged to review and check her work for careless visual errors. Routine or repetitive exercises will need special attention as she is likely to make more errors in this type of work. Improvements in her visual processing abilities, sustained attention, and visual memory may be achieved through cognitive training exercises.

Stamina
The Stamina scale is a measure of the individual's ability to sustain her speed of response time during the course of the test.

This individual's **Auditory Stamina** quotient scale score of 98 fell in the average range. This person's response time to auditory stimuli did not change significantly over the course of the test. She was able to maintain her mental processing speed in the auditory domain during the test. In a school setting, she is likely to be capable of meeting the demand to perform and to achieve goals in a timely manner.

She had an average **Visual Stamina** quotient scale score of 109. This person's response time to visual stimuli did not change significantly over the course of the test. She was able to maintain her mental processing speed in the visual domain during the test. However, she did demonstrate problems with her visual processing speed which was severely impaired. While she was able to maintain her visual stamina, she still exhibited difficulties in her ability to respond quickly overall. This deficit indicates that she is likely to have problems at times completing her school tasks within the available time allotted.

Fine Motor Hyperactivity
The Fine Motor Hyperactivity Quotient measures off-task, spurious, impulsive, and inappropriate fine motor activity using the mouse input device. A person who is squirmy, restless, or who doodles or fiddles with small objects may score low on this scale. These kinds of response tendencies may be described as fidgetiness and restlessness. Quotient scores above the average range are considered reflective of better controlled and more self-regulated responses.

This person's **Fine Motor Hyperactivity** quotient scale score was 100. Her score fell in the average range.

This average quotient score for the Fine Motor Hyperactivity scale indicates no significant problems in fine motor hyperactivity. She is unlikely to exhibit problems with fidgety, impulsive, or off-task behavior in her home or school environment.

SYMPTOMATIC SCALES
Comprehension, Steadiness, and Reliability
The Comprehension scale is a measure of idiopathic errors both of commission and omission occurring under both low and high demand conditions.

This individual's **Auditory Comprehension** quotient scale score of 52 fell in the extremely impaired range. Severe problems were identified for this individual with respect to the **Auditory Comprehension** scale. She made a large number of idiopathic errors, showing significant trouble with test performance and difficulties in following the test rules.

Her **Auditory Steadiness** quotient scale score was 35. This quotient score fell in the extremely impaired range. This impairment is very likely to impact her ability to respond appropriately to auditory stimuli when the demand to perform is high. This individual's performance on both the Auditory Comprehension and Steadiness scales reflects gross attentional dysfunction to auditory stimuli.

On the **Auditory Reliability** scale, she had a quotient score of 95. This quotient score was in the average range. She did not have problems with respect to the Auditory Reliability scale. She avoided making an excessive number of impulsive idiopathic errors of commission. She was found to show good self-control and did not react in an impulsive manner to auditory stimuli under low demand conditions.

This individual's **Visual Comprehension** quotient scale score of 83 fell in the mildly impaired range. Her Comprehension scale showed some problems with functioning and performing adequately on the IVA2 test. These difficulties led to a mild degree of idiopathic errors during the test. Her response pattern suggests that she has some problems related to comprehension that may possibly affect her.

Her **Visual Steadiness** scale was mildly to moderately impaired with a quotient score of 77. Her Visual Steadiness scale reflected significant issues indicating possible lapses in visual attention during the more demanding periods of the test when the targets are prevalent.

On the **Visual Reliability** scale, she had a quotient score of 108. This quotient score was in the average range. She did not have problems with respect to the Visual Reliability scale. She did not make an excessive number of impulsive visual idiopathic errors of commission.

Persistence

The Persistence Scale is one of the three Symptomatic scales and is used to compare the speed of simple reaction time at the beginning of the test to that measured at the end of the test.

This individual's **Auditory Persistence** quotient scale score of 89 fell in the slightly impaired range. She was slower in her auditory reaction time during the Cool-down as compared to the Warm-up period. This slower reaction time after the main section of the IVA2 test indicates the possibility of some motor or mental fatigue for auditory stimuli. However, given the range that her Auditory Persistence score fell in, her slower processing speed during the Cool-down period is not considered a significant factor that would impact her auditory test performance or her functioning in life related to auditory processing.

This person's **Visual Persistence** quotient scale score of 91 fell in the average range. No significant difference was found in her visual reaction time during the Cool-down as compared to the Warm-up. Thus, her quotient score on the Persistence scale did not indicate any problems with her motivation that would impact her functioning on the IVA2 test. Given that her Visual Stamina quotient score fell in the average range, she was not found to show any mental or motoric fatigue in respect to her ability to respond to visual stimuli. This pattern of responding indicates that she is not likely to become easily fatigued when she has to process visual stimuli.

Sensory/Motor
The Sensory/Motor scale provides a measure of an individual's simple reaction time.

This individual's **Auditory Sensory/Motor** quotient scale score of 114 fell in the above average range. This scale score was computed based on the mean of the three fastest reaction times of her auditory responses during the Warm-up test period. Her auditory simple reaction time was faster than most peers her age. This above average score on the Sensory/Motor scale indicates that she is likely to be able to process and respond quickly to auditory stimuli.

This person's **Visual Sensory/Motor** quotient scale score of 102 was in the average range. The mean of her three fastest visual reaction times during the Warm-up test period was used in determining this scale score. This individual's visual simple reaction time revealed her to be similar in performance to most other people her age.

IVA2 DIAGNOSTIC CONSIDERATIONS

This individual's pattern of responding was indicative of impairments likely to impact her functioning in the home and school settings. The global Full Scale Attention quotient scale score indicated a moderate to severe impairment. In addition, there were three Attention Primary scales that fell in the substantially impaired range.

RESOURCE LIST

IEP/504/Independent Services Plans
www.understood.org
www.nea.org/resource-library/know-your-rights-section-504-rehabilitation-act
www.greatschools.org/gk/articles/section-504-2/
www.greatschools.org/gk/articles/what-is-an-iep/
www.ed.gov for information from the U.S. Department of Education
https://www.additudemag.com/504-plan-for-adhd-accommodations-at-school/

Information on Neurofeedback
https://isnr.org/visitor-landing
www.conniemcreynolds.com

FURTHER READING SUGGESTIONS

For those who are curious to learn more about some of the topics discussed in this book, you may find the following books to be of interest.

Books About How the Brain Can Change:

Church, D. (2018). *Mind to Matter.* Carlsbad, CA: Hay House, Inc.

Doidge, N. (2007). *The Brain that Changes Itself.* New York: NY: Penguin Books

Doidge, N. (2016). *The Brain's Way of Healing.* New York: NY: Penguin Books

Helmstetter, S. (2013). *The Power of Neuroplasticity.* Gulf Breeze, FL: Park Avenue Press

Robbins, J. (2008). A *Symphony in the Brain.* New York: NY: Grove Press

Books to Better Understand the ADHD Diagnosis Process

Hinshaw, S.P. & Scheffler, R.M. (2014). *The ADHD Explosion.* New York: Oxford University Press

Saul, R. (2014). *ADHD Does Not Exist.* New York, NY: HarperCollins Publishers

Swingle, P.G. (2015). *When the ADHD Diagnosis is Wrong.* Santa Barbara, CA: Praeger

Books to Enhance Positive Well-being

Helmstetter, S. (2017). *What to Say When You Talk to Yourself*. New York, NY: Gallery Books

Helmstetter, S. (2014). *Who Are You Really and What Do You Want?* Gulf Breeze, FL: Park Avenue Press

Books on Parenting Tips

Nolte, D.L. & Harris, R. (1998). *Children Learn What They Live*. New York: NY: Workman Publishing

Siegel, D.J. & Hartzell, M. (2014). *Parenting from the Inside Out*. New York: NY: Tarcher Perigee

Excellent Book to Understand Effects of Trauma on the Body

van der Kolk, B. (2014). *The Body Keeps the Score*. New York, NY: Penguin Books

REFERENCES

Chapter 2 – Understanding the Real Cause

1. Norman, D.A. (1982). *Memory and attention: An introduction to human information processing* (2nd ed.). New York, NY: Wiley

2. Norman (1982)

3. McReynolds, C.J., Villalpando, L.S., & Britt, C.E. (2018). Using neurofeedback to improve ADHD symptoms in school-aged children. *NeuroRegulation*, 5(4), 109–128. https://dx.doi.org/10.15540/nr.5.4.109

4. Sparks. S.D. (2011). Study: Third Grade Reading Predicts Later High School Graduation http://blogs.edweek.org/edweek/inside-school-research/ 2011/04/ the_ disquieting_ side_ effect_of.html

5. Hernandez, D.J. (2011). Double jeopardy: How third-grade reading skills and poverty influence high school graduation. Annie E. Casey Foundation.

6. Hernandez (2011)

7. Hernandez (2011)

8. Sparks (2011)

9. Hernandez (2011)

10. Dillon, S. (2009). Study Finds High Rate of Imprisonment Among Dropouts https://www.nytimes.com/2009/10/09/education/09drop-out.html?

11. McReynolds (2018)

Chapter 3 – Misunderstanding the Problem

1. McReynolds, C.J., Villalpando, L.S. & Britt, C.E. (2018). Using neurofeedback to improve ADHD symptoms in school-aged children. *NeuroRegulation*, 5(4), 109–128. https://dx.doi.org/10.15540/nr.5.4.109

2. Saul, R. (2014). *ADHD Does Not Exist*. New York, NY: HarperCollins Publishers.

3. Lee, S.S., Lahey, B.B., Owens, E.B. & Hinshaw, S.P. (2008). Few preschool boys and girls with ADHD are well-adjusted during adolescence. *Journal of Abnormal Child Psychology, 36*(3), 373–383. https://dx.doi.org/10.1007/s10802-007-9184-6

4. Owens, E.B., Hinshaw, S.P., Lee, S.S. & Lahey, B.B. (2009). Few girls with childhood attention-deficit/hyperactivity disorder show positive adjustment during adolescence. *Journal of Clinical Child & Adolescent Psychology, 38*(1), 132–143. https://dx.doi.org/10.1080/15374410802575313

5. Fleming, M., Fitton, C.A., Steiner, M.F.C., McLay, J.S., Clark, D., King, A., … Pell, J.P. (2017). Educational and health outcomes of children treated for attention-deficit/ hyperactivity disorder. *JAMA Pediatrics*, 171(7). https://dx.doi.org/10.1001/jamapediatrics.2017.0691

6. Fletcher, J.M. (2014). The effects of childhood ADHD on adult labor market outcomes. *Health Economics*, 23(2), 159–181.

7. Groenman, A.P., Janssen, T.W.P., & Oosterlaan, J. (2017). Childhood psychiatric disorders as risk factor for subsequent substance abuse: A meta-analysis. *Journal of the American Academy of Child and Adolescent Psychiatry*, 56(7), 556–569.

8. Molina, B.S.G., Hinshaw, S.P., Arnold, L.E., Swanson, J.M., Pelham, W.E., Hechtman, L., … Marcus, S. (2013). Adolescent substance use in the Multimodal Treatment study of Attention-Deficit/Hyperactivity Disorder (ADHD) (MTA) as a function of childhood ADHD, random assignment to childhood treatments,

and subsequent medication. *Journal of the American Academy of Child and Adolescent Psychiatry*, 52(3), 250–263.

9. Ros, R. & Graziano, P.A. (2017). Social functioning in children with or at risk for attention deficit/hyperactivity disorder: A meta-analytic review. *Journal of Clinical Child and Adolescent Psychology*, 1–23. https://dx.doi.org/10.1080/15374416.2016.1266644

10. Grohol, J.M., (2013). Is ADHD overdiagnosed? Yes & no. Retrieved May 2016 from http://psychcentral.com/blog/archives/2013/11/21/is-adhd-overdiagnosed-yes-no/

11. Visser, S.N., Zablotsky, B., Holbrook, J.R., Danielson, M.L. & Bitsko, R.H. (2015). Diagnostic experiences of children with attention-deficit/hyperactivity disorder. *National Health Statistics Reports; 81*, 1–7. Hyattsville, MD: National Center for Health Statistics.

12. Danielson, M., Bitsko, R.H., Ghandour, R.M., Holbrook, J.R., Kogan, M.D., & Blumberg, S.J. (2018). Prevalence of Parent-Reported ADHD Diagnosis and Associated Treatment Among U.S. Children and Adolescents, 2016. *Journal of Clinical Child & Adolescent Psychology, 47*(2), 199–212, 2018 ISSN: 1537-4416 print/1537-4424 https://dx.doi.org/10.1080/15374416.2017.1417860

13. Fabiano, G.A., Pelham, W.E., Coles, E K., Gnagy, E.M., Chronis-Tuscano, A., & O'Connor, B.C. (2009). A meta-analysis of behavioral treatments for attention-deficit/ hyperactivity disorder. *Clinical Psychology Review, 29*(2), 129–140. https://dx.doi.org/10.1016/j.cpr.2008.11.001

14. Sonuga-Barke, E.J.S., Brandeis, D., Cortese, S., Daley, D., Ferrin, M., Holtmann, M., ... European ADHD Guidelines Group. (2013). Nonpharmacological interventions for ADHD: Systematic review and meta-analyses of randomized controlled trials of dietary and psychological treatments. *The American Journal of Psychiatry, 170*(3), 275–289. https://dx.doi.org/10.1176/appi.ajp.2012.12070991

15. Danielson (2018)

16. Fabiano (2009)

17. Daley, D., van der Oord, S., Ferrin, M., Danckaerts, M., Doepfner, M., Cortese, S., & Sonuga-Barke, E.J.S. (2014). Behavioral interventions in attention-deficit/hyperactivity disorder: A meta-analysis of randomized controlled trials across multiple outcome domains. *Journal of the American Academy of Child & Adolescent Psychiatry, 53*(8), 835–847.e5. https://dx.doi.org/10.1016/j.jaac.2014.05.013

18. Ellis, M. (2016, March 3). "ADHD medication and low bone density: Are kids at risk?" *Medical News Today*. Retrieved May 30, 2016, from https://www.medicalnewstoday.com/articles/307389.php

19. Brazier, Y. (2015, November 25). "ADHD medication: Is it a good idea?" *Medical News Today*. Retrieved May 2016 from https://www.medicalnewstoday.com/articles/303090.php

20. Poulton, A.S., Melzer, E., Tait, P., Garnett, S.P., Cowell, C.T., Baur, L.A. & Clarke, S. (2013). Growth and pubertal development in adolescent boys on stimulant medication for attention deficit hyperactivity disorder. *The Medical Journal of Australia, 198*(1), 29–32. https://dx.doi.org/10.5694/mja12.10931

21. MTA Cooperative Group. (2004). National Institute of Mental Health multimodal treatment study of ADHD follow-up: Changes in effectiveness and growth after the end of treatment. *Pediatrics, 113*(4), 762–769.

22. Swanson, J.M., Arnold, L.E., Molina, B.S.G., Sibley, M.H., Hechtman, L.T., Hinshaw, S.P., ... for the MTA Cooperative Group. (2017). Young adult outcomes in the follow-up of the multimodal treatment study of attention-deficit/hyperactivity disorder: Symptom persistence, source discrepancy, and height suppression. *The Journal of Child Psychology and Psychiatry, 58*(6), 663–678. https://dx.doi.org/10.1111/jcpp.12684

23. Hoagwood, K., Jensen, P., Feil, M., Vitiello, B. & Bhatpara, V. (2000). Medication management of stimulants in pediatric practice settings: a national perspective. *Journal of Developmental Behavioral Pediatrics, 21*, 322-331.

24. Gleason, M.M. (2013). Finding the tools for effective early intervention for preschool attention-deficit/hyperactivity disorder. *Journal of the American Academy of Child & Adolescent Psychiatry, 52*(3), 228–230. https://dx.doi.org/10.1016/j.jaac.2012.12.008

25. Prasad, V., Brogan, E., Mulvaney, C., Grainge, M., Stanton, W. & Sayal, K. (2013). How effective are drug treatments for children with ADHD at improving on-task behaviour and academic achievement in the school classroom? A systematic review and meta-analysis. *European Child & Adolescent Psychiatry, 22*(4), 203–216. https://dx.doi.org /10.1007/s00787-012-0346-x.

26. Swanson, J.M. & Volkow, N.D. (2009). Psychopharmacology: Concepts and opinions about the use of stimulant medications. *The Journal of Child Psychology and Psychiatry, 50*(1–2), 180–193. https://dx.doi.org/10.1111/j.1469-7610.2008.02062.x

27. Riddle, M.A., Yershova, K., Lazzaretto, D., Paykina, N., Yenokyan, G., Greenhill, L., ... Posner, K. (2013). The preschool attention deficit/hyperactivity disorder treatment study (PATS) 6-year follow-up. *Journal of the American Academy of Child & Adolescent Psychiatry, 52*(3), 264–278.e2. https://dx.doi.org/10.1016/j.jaac.2012.12.007

28. Gleason (2013)

29. American Psychiatric Association. (2013). *Diagnostic and Statistical Manual of Mental Disorders* (5th ed.). Washington, DC: Author. Retrieved from https://dx.doi.org/10.1176/appi.books.9780890425596

30. Riddle (2013)

31. Dunlop, A.J. & Newman, L.K. (2016). ADHD and psychostimulants—Overdiagnosis and overprescription. *The Medical Journal of Australia*, 204(4), 139.
https://dx.doi.org/10.5694/mja15.01387

Chapter 4 – Identifying and Treating the Root Cause

1. Woliver, R. & Ibrahim, M. (2012). *Auditory processing disorder: The hidden disability*. Long Island Press. Retrieved May 2016 from http://newideas.net/auditory-processing-disorder

2. Chronis-Tuscano, A., Molina, B.S.G., Pelham, W.E., Applegate, B., Dahlke, A., Overmeyer, M. & Lahey, B.B. (2010). Very early predictors of adolescent depression and suicide attempts in children with attention-deficit/hyperactivity disorder. *Archives in General Psychiatry, 67*(10), 1044–1051.
https://dx.doi.org/10.1001/archgenpsychiatry.2010.127

3. Hinshaw, S.P., Owens, E.B., Zalecki, C., Huggins, S.P., Montenegro-Nevada, A.J., Schrodek, E. & Swanson, E.N. (2012). Prospective follow-up of girls with attention deficit/hyperactivity disorder into early adulthood: Continuing impairment includes elevated risk for suicide attempts and self-injury. *Journal of Consulting and Clinical Psychology, 80*(6), 1041–1051.
https://dx.doi.org/10.1037/a0029451

4. Dillon, S. (2009). Study Finds High Rate of Imprisonment Among Dropouts
https://www.nytimes.com/2009/10/09/education/09dropout.html?

5. Breslau, J., Miller, E., Chung, W.J. J. & Schweitzer, J. B. (2011). Childhood and adolescent onset psychiatric disorders, substance use, and failure to graduate high school on time. *Journal of Psychiatry Research, 45*(3), 295–301.
https://dx.doi.org/10.1016/j.jpsychires.2010.06.014

6. Hinshaw, S.P. & Ellison, K. (2016). *ADHD: What everyone needs to know*. New York, NY: Oxford University Press.

7. Lee, S.S., Lahey, B.B., Owens, E.B. & Hinshaw, S.P. (2008). Few preschool boys and girls with ADHD are well-adjusted during adolescence. *Journal of Abnormal Child Psychology, 36*(3), 373–383. https://dx.doi.org/10.1007/s10802-007-9184-6

8. Owens, E.B., Hinshaw, S.P., Lee, S.S. & Lahey, B.B. (2009). Few girls with childhood attention-deficit/hyperactivity disorder show positive adjustment during adolescence. *Journal of Clinical Child & Adolescent Psychology, 38*(1), 132–143. https://dx.doi.org/10.1080/15374410802575313

9. Pingault, J.B., Tremblay, R.E., Vitaro, F., Carbonneau, R., Genolini, C., Falissard, B. & Côté, S. M. (2011). Childhood trajectories of inattention and hyperactivity and prediction of educational attainment in early adulthood: A 16-year longitudinal population-based study. *The American Journal of Psychiatry, 168*(11), 1164–1170. https://dx.doi.org/10.1176/appi.ajp.2011.10121732

Chapter 5 – How the Brain Works

1. Doidge, N. (2016). *The Brain's Way of Healing.* New York: NY: Penguin Books.

2. Doidge (2016)

3. Doidge, N. (2007). *The Brain that Changes Itself.* New York: NY: Penguin Books.

4. Doidge (2016)

5. Doidge (2007)

6. Hebb, D.O. (2002). *The Organization of Behavior: A Neuropsychological Theory* (1st ed.). Psychology Press. https://dx.doi.org/10.4324/9781410612403

7. Hebb (2002)

8. Hebb (2002)

9. Helmstetter, S. (2013). *The Power of Neuroplasticity.* Gulf Breeze, FL: Park Avenue Press.

10. McReynolds, C.J., Villalpando, L.S. & Britt, C.E. (2018). Using neurofeedback to improve ADHD symptoms in school-aged children. *NeuroRegulation, 5*(4), 109–128. https://dx.doi.org/10.15540/nr.5.4.109

11. McReynolds, C., Villalpando, L.S. & Britt, C. (2019). Identifying auditory and visual processing difficulties in school-aged children with ADHD. *Discovering New Educational Trends: A Symposium in Belize, Central America, V3.* Cambridge Scholars Publishing

12. McReynolds, C., Bell, J. & Lincourt, T.M. (2017). Neurofeedback: A noninvasive treatment for symptoms of post-traumatic stress disorder in veterans. *Journal of NeuroRegulation, 4(3-4),* 114-124. *https://dx.doi.org/10.15540/nr.4.3-4.114*

13. Doidge (2016)

14. McReynolds (2018)

15. McReynolds (2019)

16. McReynolds (2017)

17. Demos, J. (2005). *Getting Started with Neurofeedback.* New York, NY: Norton & Company.

18. Swingle, P.G. (2015). *When the ADHD Diagnosis is Wrong.* Santa Barbara, CA: Praeger.

19. Neurotransmitters. Retrieved from https://my.clevelandclinic. org/health/articles/22513-neurotransmitters

20. Neurotransmitters and their Functions. Retrieved from https://human-memory. net/ neurotransmitters/

21. Sousa, D.A. (2017). *How the Brain Learns.* 5th ed. Thousand Oaks, CA: Corwin.

22. Koepp, M.J., Gunn, R.N., Lawrence, A.D., Cunningham, V.J., Dagher, A., Jones, T. ... & Grasby, P.M. (1998). Evidence for striatal dopamine release during a video game. *Nature, 393*(6682), 266-268.

23. Greenfield, D. (2014, June/July). Video Gaming. *Neurology Now.* American Academy of Neurology.

24. Koepp (1998)

25. Paturel, A. (2014). How Do Video Games Affect Brain Development in Children and Teens? *Wellness.* (June/July). https://www.brainandlife.org/articles/how-do-video-games-affect-the-developing-brains-of-children/

26. Greenfield (2014)

27. Greenfield (2014)

28. Hummer, T.A., Wang, Y, Kronenberger, W.G., Mosier, K.M., Kalnin, A.J., Dunn, D.W. & Mathews, V.P. (2010). Short-Term Violent Video Game Play by Adolescents Alters Prefrontal Activity During Cognitive Inhibition. Published online: 11 Jun 2010. https://dx.doi.org/10.1080/15213261003799854

29. Hummer (2010)

30. Paturel (2014)

31. Greenfield (2014)

32. Hummer (2010)

33. Greenfield (2014)

34. Hummer (2010)

35. Exelmans, L., Custers, K. & Van den Bulck, J. (2015). Violent video games and delinquent behavior in adolescents: A risk factor perspective. *Aggressive Behavior*, 41: 267-279. https://dx.doi.org/10.1002/ab.21587

36. Paturel (2014)

37. Greenfield (2014)

38. Hummer (2010)

39. Greenfield (2014)

40. Greenfield (2014)

41. Paturel (2014)

42. Hummer (2010)

43. Paturel (2014)

Chapter 6 – Auditory Processing Problems

1. McReynolds, C.J., Villalpando, L.S. & Britt, C.E. (2018). Using neurofeedback to improve ADHD symptoms in school-aged children. *NeuroRegulation*, 5(4), 109–128. http://dx.doi.org/10.15540/nr.5.4.109

2. McReynolds, C., Villalpando, L.S. & Britt, C. (2019). Identifying auditory and visual processing difficulties in school-aged children with ADHD. *Discovering New Educational Trends: A Symposium in Belize, Central America, V3.* Cambridge Scholars Publishing

3. Saul, R. (2014). *ADHD Does Not Exist.* New York, NY: Harper-Collins Publishers.

4. Saul (2014)

Chapter 7 – Visual Processing Problems

1. McReynolds, C.J., Villalpando, L.S. & Britt, C.E. (2018). Using neurofeedback to improve ADHD symptoms in school-aged children. *NeuroRegulation*, 5(4), 109–128. https://dx.doi.org/10.15540/nr.5.4.109

2. Epstein, V. (2015, June 17). "Visual processing disorder: Is this what your child has?" Kars4Kids Smarter Parenting. Retrieved May 2016 from https://www.kars4kids.org/blog /visual processing-disorder-is-this-what-your-child-has

3. Epstein (2015)

4. McReynolds (2018)

5. Epstein (2015)

6. McReynolds (2018)

7. Farrar, R., Call, M. & Maples, W.C. (2001). A comparison of the visual symptoms between ADD/ADHD and normal children. *Optometry,* 72(7), 441–451.

8. Epstein (2015)

9. New Brunswick Department of Education. (1999). Resource for the identification and teaching of students with specific learning disability. Retrieved from https://www2.gnb.ca/content/dam/gnb/Departments/ed/pdf/K12/ResourceForIdentificationTeachingStudentsSpecificLearningDisability.pdf

Chapter 8 – Combined Auditory and Visual Processing Problems

1. McReynolds, C.J., Villalpando, L.S. & Britt, C.E. (2018). Using neurofeedback to improve ADHD symptoms in school-aged children. *NeuroRegulation, 5*(4), 109–128. https://dx.doi.org/10.15540/nr.5.4.109

2. Epstein, V. (2015, June 17). "Visual processing disorder: Is this what your child has?" Kars4Kids Smarter Parenting. Retrieved May 2016 from https://www.kars4kids.org/blog /visual processing-disorder-is-this-what-your-child-has

Chapter 9 – Neurofeedback and the IVA2 Assessment

1. McReynolds, C.J., Villalpando, L.S. & Britt, C.E. (2018). Using neurofeedback to improve ADHD symptoms in school-aged children. *NeuroRegulation, 5*(4), 109–128. https://dx.doi.org/10.15540/nr.5.4.109

2. Ghaziri, J., Tucholka, A., Larue, V., Blanchette-Sylvestre, M., Reyburn, G., Gilbert, G., … Beauregard, M. (2013). Neurofeedback training induces changes in white and gray matter. *Clinical EEG and Neuroscience, 44*(4), 265–272. https://dx.doi.org/10.1177/1550059413476031

3. Zhonggui, X., Shuhua, S. & Haiqing, X. (2005). A controlled study of the effectiveness of EEG biofeedback training on children with attention deficit hyperactivity disorder. *Journal of Huazhong University of Science and Technology, 25*(3), 368–370. https://dx.doi.org/10.1007/BF02828171

4. McReynolds, C., Villalpando, L.S. & Britt, C. (2019). Identifying auditory and visual processing difficulties in school-aged children with ADHD. *Discovering New Educational Trends: A Symposium in Belize, Central America, V3*. Cambridge Scholars Publishing

5. Gevensleben, H., Holl, B., Albrecht, B., Vogel, C., Schlamp, D., Kratz, O., ... Heinrich, H. (2009). Is neurofeedback an efficacious treatment for ADHD? A randomized controlled clinical trial. *Journal of Child Psychology and Psychiatry*, *50*(7), 780–789. https://dx.doi.org/10.1111/j.1469-7610.2008.02033.x

6. Gevensleben, H., Kleemeyer, M., Rothenberger, L.G., Studer, P., Flaig-Röhr, A., Moll, G. H. & Heinrich, H. (2014). Neurofeedback in ADHD: Further Pieces of the Puzzle. *Brain Topography*, *27*(1), 20–32. https://dx.doi.org/10.1007/s10548-013-0285-y

7. Hillard, B., El-Baz, A.S., Sears, L., Tasman, A. & Sokhadze, E.M. (2013). Neurofeedback Training Aimed to Improve Focused Attention and Alertness in Children with ADHD A Study of Relative Power of EEG Rhythms Using Custom-Made Software Application. *Clinical EEG and Neuroscience*, *44*(3), 193–202. https://dx.doi.org/10.1177/1550059412458262

8. Lubar, J.F. (1991). Discourse on the development of EEG diagnostics and biofeedback for attention-deficit/hyperactivity disorders. *Biofeedback and Self- Regulation*, *16*(3), 201– 225. https://dx.doi.org/10.1007/BF01000016

9. Monastra, V.J., Monastra, D.M. & George, S. (2002). The Effects of Stimulant Therapy, EEG Biofeedback, and Parenting Style on the Primary Symptoms of Attention-Deficit/ Hyperactivity Disorder. *Applied Psychophysiology and Biofeedback*, *27*(4), 231– 249. https://dx.doi.org/10.1023/A:1021018700609

10. Pop-Jordanova, N., Markovska-Simoska, S., Zorcec, T. & others. (2005). Neurofeedback treatment of children with attention deficit hyperactivity disorder. *Prilozi*, *26*(1), 71–80.

11. Sherlin, L., Arns, M., Lubar, J. & Sokhadze, E. (2010). A Position Paper on Neurofeedback for the Treatment of ADHD. *Journal of Neurotherapy, 14*(2), 66–78.
https://dx.doi.org/10.1080/10874201003773880

12. Steiner, N.J., Sheldrick, R.C., Gotthelf, D. & Perrin, E.C. (2011). Computer-based attention training in the schools for children with attention deficit/ hyperactivity disorder: A preliminary trial. *Clinical Pediatrics, 50*(7), 615–622.
https://dx.doi.org/10.1177/0009922810397887

13. Cannon, R. & Lubar, J. (2011). Long-term effects of neurofeedback training in anterior cingulate cortex: A short follow-up report, *Journal of Neurotherapy, 15*(2), 130–150.
https://dx.doi.org/10.1080/10874208.2011.570688

14. Hammond, D.C. (2011). What is neurofeedback: an update. *Journal of Neurotherapy, 15*(4), 305–336.
https://dx.doi.org /10.1080/10874208.2011.623090

15. Lubar, J.F. (1995). Neurofeedback for the management of attention-deficit/ hyperactivity disorders. In M. S. Schwartz (Ed.), *Biofeedback: A practitioner's guide* (pp. 493–522). New York, NY: Guilford Press.

16. Sandford, J.A. & Sandford, S.E. (2015). *IVA2: Integrated Visual and Auditory Continuous Performance Test Manual.* North Chesterfield, VA: Brain Train, Inc.

17. Sandford (2015)

18. Sandford (2015)

Chapter 10 – Interventions to Empower Your Child at Home and School

1. Helmstetter, S. (2017). *What to Say When You Talk to Yourself.* New York, NY: Gallery Books.

2. Helmstetter (2017)

3. Helmstetter (2017)

4. Church, D. (2018). *Mind to Matter.* Carlsbad, CA: Hay House, Inc.

5. Helmstetter (2017)

6. Helmstetter (2017)

7. Britt, C. (2022). Personal Communication.

8. Britt (2022)

Chapter 11 – Interventions for Teachers to Help Their Students

1. Britt, C. (2022). Personal Communication.

2. Britt (2022)

Chapter 12 – The Elementary School Pilot Project

1. Britt, C. (2021). The Implementation of the IVA2 and Neurofeedback as Supplementary Support for Elementary Students. [Unpublished manuscript].

2. Britt (2021)

3. Britt (2021)

4. Britt, C. (2022). Personal Communication.

Chapter 13 – Finding a Lasting Solution

1. McReynolds, C., Bell, J. & Lincourt, T M. (2017). Neurofeedback: A noninvasive treatment for symptoms of post-traumatic stress disorder in veterans. *Journal of NeuroRegulation, 4(3-4)*, 114-124. https://dx.doi.org/10.15540/nr.4.3-4.114

Appendix A – Artifact Corrected Neurofeedback

1. Sandford, J.A. (2017). SmartMind-4. BrainTrain Inc, Richmond

2. Sandford (2017)

3. La Marca, J.P, Cruz, D., Fandino, J., Cacciaguerra, F.R., Fresco, J.J. & Guerra. A.T. (2018). Evaluation of artifact-corrected

electroencephalographic (EEG) training: A pilot study. *Journal of Neural Transmission.* https://dx.doi.org/ 10.1007/ s00702-018-1877-1

4. Goncharova, I.I., McFarland, D.J., Vaughan, T.M. & Wolpaw, J.R. (2003). EMG contamination of EEG: Spectral and topographical characteristics. *Clinical Neurophysiology. 114*:1580–1593. https://dx.doi.org/10.1016/S1388-2457(03)00093-2

5. Brunner, D., Vasko, R., Detka, C., Monahan, J., Reynolds, C. III & Kupfer, D. (1996). Muscle artifacts in the sleep EEG: automated detection and effect on all-night EEG power spectra. *Journal of Sleep Research, 5*(3):155–164. https://dx.doi.org/10.1046/j.1365-2869.1996.00009.x

6. La Marca (2018)

Appendix B – Description of IVA2 Scores

1. Sandford, J.A. & Sandford, S.E. (2015). *IVA2: Integrated Visual and Auditory Continuous Performance Test Manual.* North Chesterfield, VA: Brain Train, Inc.

Appendix C – IVA2 Definitions

1. Sandford, J.A. & Sandford, S.E. (2015). *IVA2: Integrated Visual and Auditory Continuous Performance Test Manual.* North Chesterfield, VA: Brain Train, Inc.

Appendix D - Differences Between IEPs, 504 Plans, and Individual Service Plans

1. www.understood.org
2. www.nea.org/resource-library/know-your-rights-section-504-rehabilitation-act
3. www.greatschools.org/gk/articles/section-504-2/
4. www.greatschools.org/gk/articles/what-is-an-iep/

ABOUT THE AUTHOR

 Connie McReynolds, Ph.D. is a Licensed Psychologist, Certified Rehabilitation Counselor, and Certified Vocational Evaluator with more than 30 years of experience in the field of rehabilitation counseling and psychology. She earned her Ph.D. in Rehabilitation Psychology at the University of Wisconsin-Madison gaining valuable experiences in the Outpatient Substance Abuse Treatment Program at the William S. Middleton VA Hospital, at the Physical Medicine and Rehabilitation Neuropsychological Clinic at Meriter Hospital, and the Mendota Mental Health Institute.

Dr. McReynolds is Professor Emeritus and former Program Coordinator of the Rehabilitation Counseling master's degree program at California State University, San Bernardino where she worked for more than 14 years. Previously, she taught ten years at Kent State University, Ohio in the Rehabilitation Counseling master's degree program and served in numerous leadership roles. As a Fellow of the National Rehabilitation Counseling Association, she served on the Executive Committee for more than two decades advocating for individuals with disabilities. She has contributed to 40+ publications and given more than 200 presentations on a multitude of conditions and topics. She was also inducted into the Phi Kappa Phi Honor Society for scholarly distinction.

Dr. McReynolds has shared her expertise across the United States and Europe at conferences in Vienna, Oslo, Oxford University, Bucharest, Belize, Prague, London, and Toronto. She is the founder of neurofeedback clinics in southern California working with children and adults ages five to 90 to reduce or eliminate conditions of ADHD, anxiety, anger, depression, chronic pain, learning problems, and trauma.